Alfred Neumeyer—art historian, teacher, critic, author—has made the field of modern art his specialty. Among his books are studies of Cézanne, El Greco, and Albrecht Dürer. Dr. Neumeyer acted as Director of the Mills College Art Gallery between 1938 and 1961 and is now Professor of Art History there. He is a member of the board of directors of the College Art Association of America and *Honorarprofessor* at the Free University of Berlin.

Translated from the German, *Die Kunst in unserer Zeit: Versuch einer Deutung* (Stuttgart: Henry Goverts Verlag, 1961), by Ruth Angress.

The Search for Meaning
IN MODERN ART

by ALFRED NEUMEYER
Foreword by Sir Herbert Read

Prentice-Hall, Inc. A SPECTRUM BOOK Englewood Cliffs, N.J.

To Carl Georg Heise

Current printing (last digit):

12   11   10   9   8   7   6   5

FOREWORD

Art, declared Oscar Wilde in one of his aphorisms, is perfectly meaningless. Dr. Neumeyer's search for a meaning in modern art might therefore seem to be rather pointless. But art today is very different from art in Wilde's time, and it is this difference that needs explanation.

The kind of art we have in mind when we speak specifically of "modern" art is a kind of art that has rejected decisively the whole concept of art as *mimesis*, that is to say, art as some kind of representation of natural phenomena, a "mirroring" of objective realities. Modern art has renounced that aim and, although it may still make use of images derived from objective reality, it is distinct from the art of the past in its desire and ability to use nonobjective symbols as substitutes for inner states of mind. Such symbolic substitutes, though nonobjective, must still work through the senses, and for this reason they are distinct from logical symbols, which function for a rational understanding of reality. Modern art, even when most metaphysical, as in the paintings of Kandinsky and Mondrian, must still make use of sensuous images if it is to achieve its aim.

What that aim is becomes clear as we read Dr. Neumeyer's cogent analysis of architecture, sculpture, and painting. It is significant that he takes the arts in this order: there is an historical as well as a logical justification for this preference. The prehistoric period may be an exception, though even in this case the cave as a space to be occupied was an earlier concept than the designs that were then painted or engraved on the walls. In general, however, the arts of sculpture and painting developed as arts ancillary to architecture in the sequence adopted by Dr. Neumeyer for modern art. It is sometimes said (I have said it myself) that modern architecture has been influenced by modern painting, but this is true only in a superficial or decorative sense. What is fundamental in all the arts, as Dr. Neumeyer so clearly demonstrates, is the desire and ability to give shape and definition to space. The composition common to all the plastic arts is a dialectic of voids and solids: the rest is ornament.

Nevertheless the various arts must be differentiated, and here Dr. Neumeyer makes some very perceptive definitions—that, for example, a modern building is *a body in space*, whereas a piece of modern sculpture is *a creature in space*. He does not attempt to apply a similar neat categorization to all the varieties of modern expressionism in painting, but he has a poetic image which well describes the same quality in modern painting: "Between the experience of reality and the abstractions that have grown from it, a luminous space opens up, where mind and nature merge into one."

Dr. Neumeyer's book is at once comprehensive and concise. There is little that he misses in the complex panorama of modern art, and yet the reader is never lost in what he somewhere calls "the diagram of vitality." That vitality is communicated, and the author, whose pretentions are unusually modest, must be congratulated for having brilliantly fulfilled his aim, which is to *mediate* between the work of art (rather than the artist) and the public (rather than the connoisseur). He has succeeded where many have failed—in establishing the "general intelligibility" of a period of art that is often condemned for its unintelligibility.

Herbert Read

PREFACE

Where is art going from here? Will esotericism and monomania, ground on hundreds of mills, become the main staple of our age? The decision can come only from the artist, not from the critic. If we assume that breadth, abundance, power, and originality are the criteria of all genuine art, then the danger of nonrepresentational art is obviously atrophy of content. Art without reference runs the risk of becoming mere gesture, like the instinctive chirping of birds. Therefore a way must be found to give the young artist an education that will provide him with a maximum of content to take with him.

Theory of form is an end product in a long process of sifting and sorting, and it should therefore not come at the beginning of an artist's education, but should be allowed to emerge gradually from his own encounter with the surrounding world. To know the world and himself, he must first look at it, absorb it, and experience it. Besides, the experience of the visual world includes a knowledge and absorption of what art has achieved until now, an awareness of that "continuum" from which the new way of looking must arise. According to Jakob Burckhardt, it is a sign of barbarism never to break through one's own cultural shell. Awareness may be a handicap to a small talent, but a great one will be ripened and directed by it.

The education of the growing artist should, then, proceed according to his own psycho-physical development. In offering him materials, it will stake out his horizons. In recreating visual models, he will be led to the laws of visualization. In confronting the outer world, the inner man will be enriched. In recreating natural and art forms, the flux of his consciousness will acquire structure.

Precisely because the art of today has left behind it the visible world, it is of the utmost importance for the growing artist to encounter and experience this world before he goes on. If his renunciation is not the result of a struggle that leads to a higher plane of reality, it is not valuable. The work of Cézanne may serve to remind us of the painful grandeur to which the clash of nature and form may give rise. Ultimately, the problematic quality of contemporary art is due not to a subjective incomprehensibility —as we shall see, within limits it *is* comprehensible—but to its relative lack of content. If this lack of content persists and continues, then technology alone will shape the man of the future.

A. N.

CONTENTS

SCULPTURE, 43

PAINTING, 69

ILLUSTRATIONS

ARCHITECTURE

PAINTING

INTRODUCTION

The man who has never had doubts about the art of his age is to be pitied, but he who has never been able to re-live it is not aware of the pulse of his time. Questions about the significance and direction of art arise only from a sense of direct participation and involvement.

The fact that the new art is occasionally incomprehensible to a large number of people (including, at times, myself) does not speak against the sincerity and ability of those who create it; it merely proves Delacroix's observation: "Art is a clock that moves too fast when measured by the public's sense of time."

In fact, since the beginning of the modern era—approximately since the Reformation and the great sixteenth-century discoveries in geography and the natural sciences—the mutual exchange between artist and society has been blocked in certain areas. With the French Revolution, art entered a new phase.

It will not do to call this new phase a crisis. The word *crisis* implies that only one state of existence is possible—namely, the one that preceded the supposed crisis. But if art is viewed in an historical or ethnic perspective, it can be seen that its functions are extremely varied. One judge of contemporary art reveals his cogent skepticism in regard to the concept of crisis when he says: ". . . those who have talked of crises in art have invariably been those who have themselves not sufficiently penetrated the depths and mysteries of the great creative process which leads to the work of art. . . ." [1]

One of the characteristics of this so-called crisis is supposed to be a lack of general intelligibility. This lack is said to originate in the gradual disappearance of a valid image of man as he is or as he should be. However, one may raise certain objections to the assumption that general comprehensibility existed in art prior to the French Revolution. The art of a Watteau or a Boucher was created primarily for the nobility; how many nonaristocrats were able to appreciate it? Perhaps appreciation was the intellectual property of a numerically small upper class. Moreover, how many could fully understand the artistic statements of a Rembrandt or a Grünewald? And finally, how many admirers of Raphael's "Sistine Madonna" were inspired by the concept of the Madonna rather than by the work of art that represented her?

In brief, then, the "general intelligibility" of art has been limited even before our own time. First, art has always been modified by the social rank and educational background of those for whom it was created. Second, as the work of a solitary genius, art has always tended to move away from contemporary cultural realities —even to the point where the artist creates for himself worlds that have not existed before. And third, a work of art has always been exposed to the advantage—as well as to the danger—of being equated with its subject matter.

The phase which art entered after the French Revolution and particularly since the turn of the twentieth century is characterized by the comparative freedom of artistic production from the demands of a specific social group or religious community. Instead, it is now the artist who chooses, discovers, and gives shape to his subject matter and problems. As a result, there are today two opposed camps: on one side are ranged the creative artists, and *with* them —most unlike the Impressionist period—a phalanx of interpreting critics; on the other side stands the public, which does not so much condemn as ask for enlightenment, because it does not trust its own eyes and thinks of itself as uninitiated.

It can readily be seen that the situation is different from that of, say, 1870. Today, critics no longer compare the avant-garde efforts of their day with "the scribbling of idiots" [2]; contemporary criticism is either passionately or anxiously engaged in doing justice to the creations of its age, and the public no longer has the self-confidence to maintain its own opinion against that of the artist. On the contrary, art, freed from external direction and control, has achieved an independence greater than any it has known since the Italian Renaissance. From the point of view of art, this is a triumph. But if we think of culture as the totality of forces shaping human existence and consider that art used to be subordinated to these forces, this independence or detachment becomes a disquieting element. Art has assumed a position of leadership; nevertheless, we face it with an undeniable sense of discomfort and unease. Could this discomfort stem precisely from the fact that art has so obviously stepped to the center of the stage? In so doing, has it perhaps raised in many anxious hearts the question of whether it can and does fulfill the responsibilities of so central a role? Natural as this question is, it can be answered only if one takes into full account the goals of the various branches of current artistic creativity, the artistic statements they make, and the connection between these statements and the totality of our culture. Art has relinquished its relation to the visible world; therein lies its greatest challenge to our inherited concept of culture. This step is in itself so momentous that it ought to appeal to our instinct for discovery, to our need for creative adventure, with all its risks and rewards.

Today's art, obscure as it may seem at first to many observers, is closely related to the experiences and sufferings of the modern age. It cannot be altered by critical verdict. For better or for worse, art is what we are, for it is born in a setting of freedom. Inasmuch as it constitutes a new way of looking at the world, it also projects a new content. This art is precisely the "clock" that moves too fast. Other disciplines can elucidate art only to a minimal degree: Neither sociology nor psychology can explain its essentials, for its true content is inherent in its very plasticity and visibility. Lastly, art is an independent plant even though its roots are nourished by the same soil that feeds all the other creative impulses of a culture. By focusing exclusively on the work of art itself, we hope to arrive at an understanding of its form and content.

A visit to a modern art gallery is both disturbing and exhilarating. We partake of a vitality and originality that seem to emanate from a chaotic encounter. The Renaissance humanist Pico della Mirandola once said: "For what else does chaos mean but that matter is full of forms, albeit they be in a confused and imperfect state?" The artist of today expresses this confused and imperfect state of matter—and *matter* includes the artist himself. He holds the mirror up to chaos, he puts (like the doubting Thomas) his finger in the wound, and he heightens others' perception of reality through his own insight. Suffering, pain, and chaos are part of the human condition which is, and must be, shared by art if art is to be truthful and alive. Since the Book of Genesis and Hesiod, the story of the creation of the world has been told as a creation out of chaos. The art of our time is such creation.

ARCHITECTURE

Architecture gives the clearest, the most perceptible demonstration that ours is a specific and singular life situation. The inhabitants of a small town in Europe would undoubtedly be glad to keep their narrow streets, steep gables, stone façades, and picturesque nooks and crannies, but the architect does not permit them to do so. He builds what he is told to build, but he transforms purpose into shape. Contemporary buildings do not repeat what we already know; instead, they reveal something that we learn only as we look at them. Thus they teach us a new architectural language. Moreover, the architect not only expresses the present sense of existence, but he may also anticipate. In conceiving a new view of space and statics, he creates, so to speak, the stage on which future generations will play their part. While we are still laboriously spelling out the story of human experience, art turns the page and confronts us with a new chapter. But precisely because the text is new, it will be full of disjointed utterances, rash assertions, and fashionable exaggerations. This is *our* world; it is for future generations to judge how good it is. For architecture is a programmatic declaration of the will to live and of the purpose of life.

Mediterranean and medieval architecture

A walk through a city in which old buildings exist side by side with contemporary structures gives us an immediate and direct impression that modern architecture is basically different from that of the past. The first thing we notice about the new buildings is that they are taller and that they have been constructed from new materials; but much more essential is the changed conception of the building itself. Any building is determined by two factors: its function and the manner in which this function becomes visible (or blurred, as the case may be). It is this second factor which we call the *form* of a building. All too often it is assumed that the two are identical. Yet stylistic vitality may prove stronger than the function and triumphantly ignore it as something merely utilitarian, or the artist may be incapable of formulating the changed function or too tradition-bound to express it. Vitruvius demanded in the name of *proprietas* that form and function be one, but neither the Augustan period in which Vitruvius was active nor the age of eclecticism adhered to this demand. Usually more vital qualities than utilitarianism have influenced architecture. The mere instinct to build produces the bird's nest and the beehive, but it is the drive toward the formal arrangement of matter in space that raises architecture beyond utility to an art. The outer appearance of the Greek temple, the Renaissance palace, and their Baroque successor does not reveal their inner spatial form—their function. On the contrary, the façades have an identity of their own, presenting—with their own proportions and ornaments—a self-contained image. Such is the basic tendency of classical architecture. Opposed to this tendency stands the functionally unified building, in which the interior suggests the shape of the exterior. The early Christian basilicas (although derived from Graeco-Roman origins) are the first example of this type of building which achieved its highest triumphs in the Gothic cathedral but which later, during the Baroque Age, blended with the Mediterranean, façade-oriented style.

Buildings of classical origin—whether they be Roman temples, Renaissance palaces, or Baroque structures—display anthropomorphic proportions and measurements. Their rhythmic order has an almost musical effect and their geometric lucidity enlightens, as it were, the mind and senses of the viewer.

If we then turn to a medieval castle or a Gothic cathedral, we are struck by the difference. Instead of one unified image which presents itself immediately and fully to the eye, there is now a structure that yields only to a slowly emerging insight and allows us to penetrate but gradually. The observer wants to walk around the building; in doing so, he discovers new formal structures and develops a sense of awareness for an architectural organism that has more than one appearance. However, what he has seen is not merely a utilitarian, functional building, even though the interior has had more influence on its over-all development than is the case with the classical edifice. Its specific use—religious or residential—inspires the formal execution and brings into view its vital forces through alcoves, pinnacles, towers, and rose windows. The measure of these buildings is not man alone, nor is the impression they make on the eye solely geometric. The will toward expression, constantly nourished by the function of the building, leads to a symbolic visualization of the vital and spiritual forces contained therein. For such an architecture, the façade is only a part—only *one* aspect—of a building that has many facets and many meanings.

Modern architecture: plasticity in space

This historical digression was necessary to make clear that one encounters an entirely new configuration in contemporary architecture. We all perceive this difference but we rarely give it conscious consideration because the difference lies neither in the new materials nor in the architectural expression of the building's function—even though the function may be unique to our time. What we see before us is no longer an embodiment of the well-known geometric shapes—rectangle, square, circle, or oval—that used to be the basis of all of Occidental architecture but, rather, the presentation of shapes which had not existed before. The proportions of these buildings are no longer related to the human form, and their shape is not exclusively that of Euclidean geometry; instead, architecture now enriches the world with configurations and syntheses which, like those of contemporary painting, are completely novel.

Let us consider such a pleasantly fashionable structure as a linoleum store in Milan (Figure I). All of us have seen any number of such stores, hotel lobbies, or restaurants. Without our being fully conscious of it, their "style" has already profoundly affected our conception of space and form. Their freely balanced, irregular, abstract forms have brought Cubist vision into the everyday world. Floating and hanging stairs, ceilings, and roofs have changed our relationship to the flat ground as well as to perspective and to space. It is true that these novel configurations would be unthinkable unless they fulfilled a practical purpose for, in fact, it is the purpose that feeds the architect's imagination. Nevertheless, purpose and imagination are by no means identical.

ARCHITECTURE

As in all great architectural periods, the will to create reaches beyond the task at hand.

Much has been written about the functionalism of modern architecture, which is said to have originated with Walter Gropius' Bauhaus in Dessau (1926). This magnificent work, however, was ridden with functional flaws from the very beginning. For example, the glass front of the entrance wall has brought about an unusual degree of heat in summer and cold in winter. Surely this façade is not explained by the purpose of the building; rather, it is the fulfillment of an architect's dream, a dream that envisioned the envelopment of a building with a floating, weightless veil at once transparent and opaque. Even the term *façade* loses its justification, for the complex consists of three buildings and presents more than one main view. There is no "front" and "back" view, for the building radiates in many directions and can be grasped only if one walks around it. In the same way the thirty-storied apartment houses of Mies van der Rohe in Chicago (1949-51; II) are primarily the fulfillment of an architectural dream which had existed on paper as early as 1920. The purity of the aesthetic solution seems as insurpassable as that of the Parthenon. (Perhaps the priests of that temple complained about its darkness or its cramped inner space much as today's inhabitants of the glass towers may complain of cold, vertigo, and storm psychoses.) Finally, the same observation can be made with regard to the houses built by America's great architect, Frank Lloyd Wright. For several of these it was necessary to build trapezoidal and triangular beds, chairs, and tables to fit his star-shaped and trapezoidal interiors. But at a certain point the human body can no longer keep step with the bold, plastic imagination of the artist-architect and regretfully has to admit its physiological limitations.

We have come to the heart of the matter: the driving force behind modern architecture is its plastic imagination—hence the

ARCHITECTURE   **eleven**

peculiar expressive energy of the projections and recessions, the vehement speed of its vertical lines, the rhythmic intensity of its horizontals. This motivating power of plastic energy becomes very clear when we go back to the beginnings of the new style—for example, to Frank Lloyd Wright's so-called prairie houses, which were built near Chicago in the early years of this century. The blueprint of the Robie House in Chicago (1909-1910; III) resembles the design for an abstract geometric painting in the manner of the Constructivists (van Doesburg, Albers, Moholy-Nagy). An arrangement of cubes along a horizontal axis prevails and develops its own energy and rhythm of form. The characteristic plasticity is manifested in the interpenetration of the vertical and the horizontal elements. The free, mobile beauty of this floor plan has its counterpart in the roof, the balcony, and the joining walls, which become, as it were, plastic events in space. At the base of Le Corbusier's skyscraper, the *Unité d' Habitation*, in Marseilles, the element of decoration appears as part of the structure itself (IV). Here architecture, sculpture, and decoration are no longer separable, for each is part of the others. On the other hand, a self-contained ornament may still add decoration as well as significance to a building, as Henry Moore has shown in the Time-Life building in London (1952). In this case, the ornament becomes, as it were, a metamorphosis of the wall, much as the caryatids on the Erechtheion are metamorphoses of columns.

Louis Sullivan, the beloved master of Wright, himself a creative designer of ornaments, was perhaps the first to point out this tendency of the modern age when he stated that ". . . it would be greatly for our aesthetic good if we should refrain entirely from the use of ornament for a period of years in order that our thought might concentrate acutely upon the production of building well formed and comely in the nude." [3] The Viennese architect Adolf Loos, who presumably did not know Sullivan, passionately defended the same point of view: "The road of culture is a

III. Wright, Robie House (1909-1910), Chicago

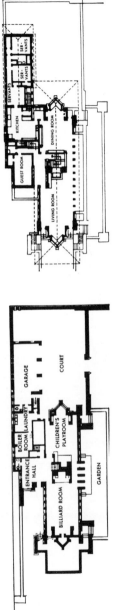

IV. Le Corbusier, *Unité d'Habitation* (1943-1950), Marseilles

ARCHITECTURE   fourteen

road away from ornament toward the absence of ornament. Evolution in culture is synonymous with the removal of ornaments from functional objects. . . . The aim of all mankind is to look for beauty only in form and to make beauty independent of decoration." [4] Loos arrived at this opinion solely on aesthetic grounds. But his statement gains in significance when we consider that ornaments used to have religious and magical overtones before they became purely aesthetic objects. As man moves away from a supernatural world view, his aesthetics must become more "objective," and his emphasis will be less on the mark of distinction (that is, the decoration) and more on the object itself. Thus, the thesis advanced by Loos may be buttressed with evidence adduced from anthropology and cultural history.

However, the antidecorative attitude, too, is already a thing of the past. Ornaments have once again begun to appear on buildings during the last decade, but they are no longer superimposed on the building, as they used to be; rather, they have become an integral part of the structure itself.

The International Style

This intensification of plasticity was introduced by the masters of the so-called International Style—Gropius, Mies van der Rohe, Neutra, Aalto, and Breuer—and demonstrated by them with almost ascetic restraint on cube-like structures. Buildings as well as furniture (for example, the Breuer chair), were reduced to a minimum of matter and kept free of decoration, so that every line could be developed with maximum clarity. The interaction of lines, in turn, then developed into a body in space—a body distinguished by the utmost precision of outline.

The essence of Gropius architecture may be observed as early as his first building, the Fagus shoe factory in Alfeld-an-der-Leine (1910-11), which he designed with Adolf Meyer. Here, for the first time, glass walls are joined without vertical supports and give the impression of a weightless glass skin. Because the actual supports have been transferred to the interior, the wall could now be made into a transparent cover. Gropius developed this technique further, after 1919, in the theory and architecture of the Bauhaus.

The architectural theory of the Bauhaus, as presented by Gropius, Marcel Breuer, and others put the greatest stress on establishing an intimate contact with the Machine Age and on exploring the means of mechanical production and the basic shapes resulting from it. When Gropius, Mies van der Rohe, and Breuer were forced by Hitler to leave Germany, the new theory emigrated with them to the New World. With emphatic and ascetic strictness they carried out what William Morris and Henry van de Velde had initiated: they paid attention to the working processes, to the appropriateness of the materials, to the dignity of functional aims, and to the creation of a purposeful order. "The long journey from raw material via function to the finished artistic shape has only one goal: we want to bring order to the surrounding world." [5] The great pioneers of the new architecture pursued this idea of order with an intensity that carried them far beyond the concept of functionalism. According to Le Corbusier: "We may say that the farther human creations move away from what is directly tangible, the more they tend toward pure geometry. A violin or a chair which touches our bodies are of a lesser geometry, but the city is pure geometry. When man is free, he will choose pure geometry; he will create what is known as order." [6] But even the staunchest adherents of geometric order allowed their work to be influenced by their creative vitality.

It is not an accident that Klee, Kandinsky, and Feininger, masters of an art that was approaching music, taught simultaneously at the Bauhaus. The Bauhaus could not have become the most influential art school of the twentieth century if the paintings of these masters had not had something in common with the ideals

of the architects and if Gropius had not therefore sensed an affinity in them. What the two fields share is a drive toward absolute form. Until then, painting had been bound to the objective world; architecture, to a Mediterranean classical or a Northern, medieval tradition. The concepts that led painters to the exploration of new color spaces or line tensions and the interpenetration of space and surface planes led architects to the exploration of new plastic shapes in space. The functionalism of the Bauhaus is not purely utilitarian but, rather, a demonstration of new tasks and human situations; it appeals not so much because it fulfills a function as because it interprets it. Unfettered by tradition, it exerts plastic energy in space. This is its unique property.

Le Corbusier and Wright

Le Corbusier and Frank Lloyd Wright are poets of space whose imaginations tend toward all-embracing concepts. Challenged by an architectural task, they carry it to its boldest and most startling limits. Whereas the United Nations building in New York (built in 1950 by an international advisory committee of architects coordinated by Wallace K. Harrison) resembles a glass cube whose function can in no manner be deduced from the exterior, Wright's buildings are comparable to works of sculpture which must be grasped and understood in their entirety. The void and its shell are the given factors from which Wright created an apparently flexible shape such as the Johnson Wax Building in Racine, Wisconsin (1936-39). The center is compact, the rounded corners are inflated with space, and the whole seems to function freely, like a living organism (V). Wright's own architectural atelier, Taliesin West (Arizona, 1938-59), shows how landscape evoked in him an architectural counterimage, not necessarily flawless in execution, but magnificent in total conception. It looks as if it had sprung from the earth itself: the lower part derives from the tradition of the Spanish-Indian adobe house; above, wooden rafters hold the canvas roof like parallel, oblique clamps. Every Wright building emphasizes either the concordance or the juxtaposition of architecture and landscape. In this respect, his achievement is unique. Wright was one of the greatest pioneers in applying modern means to the process of creating shapes in space, even though a romantic feeling for the effect of a given locale tied him to the nineteenth century, from which he inherited his somewhat theatrical perception of nature and the ego as well as the decorative effects of his interiors.

The fundamental concept of Wright's buildings does not spring from their function, but from his integrated vision of exterior and interior which, in turn, were fitted into the context of countryside or city. Although, in the process of design, the triumphant imagination of the architect often overstepped the needs of the inhabitants, the same may be said of many of the great buildings of the Renaissance and the Baroque periods, as a glance at the floor plan of Palladio's Villa Rotunda in Vicenza will prove.

In contrast to Wright's romanticism is Le Corbusier's extreme rationalism, which broadened only gradually. In his first plans for a concrete house (about 1915), he reduced the building to its basic shape: a cube open to light. With the Villa Savoye in Poissy (1928-30), he introduced a type of building that rests on free-standing supports. When he designed the Swiss Dormitory at the University City in Paris (1930-32), he produced the same effect of a freely floating building, but on a larger scale. Since the skeleton alone holds the structure of the building, the interior walls are independent of the exterior and the rooms may be arranged with utmost liberty. Thus, two strangely opposed trends meet: under the impact of Cubism, the body of the building becomes a rigid geometric figure while the interior subdivisions dissolve, fuse, and merge with one another.

The principle of freely floating buildings is now generally established. A building no longer has to "grow"; instead, its parts can be spanned and tied across a skeleton in free motion. Much as abstract painting has abandoned the ground line as a point of departure in composition, so architecture attempts to detach the building from its base. The two developments are clearly related. Le Corbusier has remained loyal to this fundamental form: sculptural parts, which used to occupy only a minor place, have broadened in importance to the point where they are now equal to the geometric structure itself.

Beyond Euclidean geometry

The idea that a structure could be riveted and spanned across a skeleton led to the construction of cube-shaped buildings—a style that was perfected (and adhered to with the greatest consistency) by Ludwig Mies van der Rohe. At one time, the fundamental visual experience offered by a building was an architectural demonstration of weights and supports. Since the substitution of concrete and metal for stone and brick, this is no longer true. Instead, the impression is now one of weightless, transparent, or mirror-like surfaces; the curtain-wall has become a dominant feature of contemporary architecture. The aesthetic statement is conveyed by even arrangement of openings, rhythmic repetition, and proportional relations, but the statement itself is impersonal or superpersonal. The new buildings mirror the activity of man, but they do not symbolize its power; rather, they demonstrate its processes. There is something frightening as well as sublime to this uniformity. The individual seems to have been extinguished, but the sum of individuals is overwhelming. The architectural expression of power has been split into its constituent elements, and the building speaks not of ordered mass, but of organized units.

The biomorphic style

During the last decade there has developed an opposition to—or at least a wider interpretation of—constructivistic architecture.

This expansion has led to biomorphic methods of construction, in which swelling forms replace flat surfaces. One of the causes for this development is to be found in the employment of concrete and steel; the rest is due to an antimechanistic conception of architecture.

Let us start with the constructivistic elements in the work of the engineer-architect Pier Luigi Nervi. In his sport arenas and airplane hangars, there appears for the first time an architecture of soaring curves. Here the constructive imagination has taken as its point of departure the stairway and roof, which are not bound to the horizontal-vertical system, and has fused their shapes with that of the entire building, including the outer covering. The use of concrete, steel, and rivets permits the development of a beehive or rib structure, and the total effect is one of weightless, floating forms. Similarly, the roofs over the stands of the racing course of La Zarzuela (Madrid), built by Eduardo Torroja in 1935, demonstrate how space can be delimited by means of a thin shell.

This fusion of technology and aesthetics has been adopted by those architects who think of their work as more or less analogous to nature. Such a conception of architecture, diametrically opposed to the Mediterranean tradition, can be found as early as Art Nouveau and Jugendstil, or in the buildings of Gaudí in Barcelona. Frank Lloyd Wright's adherence to this theory in the early 1920's is manifested in the "hollow honeycomb" design he developed for the interior floor plan and elevation of several of his houses, such as the Millard House in Pasadena (1923). Only in his late work did Wright's theories reach their fullest manifestation. His last work, the Guggenheim Museum in New York (1958-60), is a good example (VI). A spiral ramp rises around the rim of the circular interior—the pure embodiment of the snail house which was one of Wright's artistic ideals. Hollow space and solid mantle correspond in form; space is in continuous

ARCHITECTURE   **twenty-two**

movement throughout the interior, flowing toward all sides. The architect may have neglected some of the specific needs of the museum, but although functionally imperfect, the building remains a magnificent realization of tectonics. Perhaps this "Michelangelo conflict" of pure form versus use has to be borne by all great visionaries in art.

In Le Corbusier a rationalistic—and hence geometric—architectural intensity has made a strange pact with a versatile gift for creating plastic shapes. In the Swiss Dormitory of the University City of Paris, he gave a concave shape to the concrete pilotis (supports), recessing them deeply under the great structural mass. Later, when he designed the *Unité d' Habitation* in Marseilles (1947-52), he divided a row of twenty-five balconies by placing a wall between each adjacent pair, thus producing the impression of a rectangular honeycomb. The idea, originally a functional one, became a decorative element of the façade in the Indian administrative capital, Chandigarh (1951-   ). Le Corbusier wanted to invigorate the cubic skeleton building by adding plasticity and shadow. He thus restored dimensionality to the International Style, not by working in analogy to natural organisms, as Wright did, but by adapting the sculptural abstractions introduced in the early 1920's by his contemporaries, such as Lipchitz and Arp. Finally, with the church of Ronchamp (1950-55), Le Corbusier made of a building a completely abstract work of art (**IX**, below). There is no longer such a thing as a "main" view, for if one is to grasp its shape, the building must be studied as an abstract sculpture from all sides. The roof folds upward like a curling leaf, resting on a keel or spur, as if it were a creature come to rest for only a moment. Inside the church there is an almost medieval lyricism of space and light. The walls seem perforated by the light which penetrates through irregular, deep openings. Le Corbusier has increasingly tended to "loosen up" his architectural cubism—a tendency that has also guided the Brazilian architect Oscar Niemeyer toward bold, although frequently playful, formations.

The use of concrete enables the architect to apply the forms of baldachin, net, and drum to gigantic constructions. With this innovation, we come to a significant phenomenon: the new architecture has given rise to plastic ornament that is not imposed on the building but is part of the building itself. The Cosmic Radiation Laboratory of the University of Mexico (1952; **VII**), designed by Felix Candela, is a functional building of beautiful simplicity that may serve as an example. The powerful lines of the ground supports and the roof constitute a single graphic pattern, while the corrugated wall translates the curvature into a plastic, wavy ornament. In this new way of animating the surface plane, the ornamental principle is provided by the function. Another example can be found in Oscar Niemeyer's presidential palace in Brasilia, in which concrete supports connected by curving arches rise toward the roof they seem to support (**VIII**). In Eero Saarinen's TWA terminal at New York's Kennedy Airport, the parabolic curves of the engines seem to have turned into a spectacle of space.

These examples are all very imaginative indeed, but we may well ask whether we are not witnessing the beginnings of a new Beaux Arts revival which pretends to be functional but actually is not. A new type of sculptural architecture is quietly coming to life. Its roots, to be sure, are chiefly nourished by Bauhaus objectivity, but it might turn into the very antithesis of the Bauhaus principle. The intentions that are expressed in the parabolic curves of these walls and roofs are nothing but architectural symbols for a new feeling of life. This feeling is expressed in the demonstration of the possibilities of the new building materials, the wish to break with architectural tradition, the creation of an architectural world of art which sets itself up against the world of nature, and finally the creation of buildings that are suspended from skeletons and thus seem almost to float above the ground.

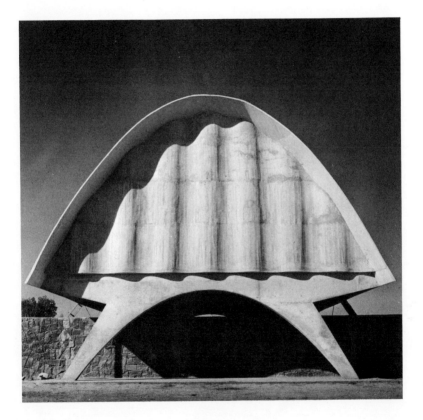

ARCHITECTURE

twenty-five

VIII. Niemeyer, Presidential Palace (1958-1960), Brasilia, Brazil

Nevertheless, architecture has as its social function the fulfillment of practical requirements. The new interaction of creative purpose with the limitations imposed by these practical tasks has given rise to a reciprocal intensification of each, and also to theatrical poses, in which form and function bypass one another. There are definite limits for an architectural art that would go beyond the international style. The never-ending challenge will lie in the problem of fusing form and function.

So far we have discussed architecture as if it were solely the product of the creative instincts of individual masters. But although the tasks set by a culture are chiefly recognized and solved by outstanding individuals, each age poses the problems which its architects must solve, and these problems, to some extent, themselves determine the style of their solution.

Fluid architectural structure: nature and architecture

We have seen that the leading architects of our time tend to reduce the material limitations imposed by their media. A related tendency is to "loosen up" the ground plan of individual buildings and, even more frequently, of a group of buildings. There can be found sets of regulations, dating from as far back as the late sixteenth century, which the Spanish government prepared for its American settlements. These regulations stipulate that light and weather conditions must be considered in building human habitations, that slaughtering houses must be built at the edge of the settlements, and set forth similar rules designed to protect the health of the inhabitants. Such centralized planning is feasible only under absolute monarchies and dictatorships; democratic administrations proceed more slowly and their solutions are frequently the product of compromise.

In many countries, the problem has been aggravated by the fact that the prospect of better earnings and a higher living standard has drawn the rural population to the city, thus increasing urban congestion and providing fuel for the financial machinations of real estate speculators and unscrupulous landlords.

Nothing will illustrate this situation more clearly than an aerial photograph of New York City. The nineteenth-century drive to build on every available foot of the narrow island of Manhattan seemed designed to assure the millions of inhabitants a slow death by suffocation. The colossal and terrifying appearance of certain parts of this city is not created by the towering skyscrapers alone, but by the crowded tenements that display the monumental callousness of such uninhibited and unplanned building. Children slouch along ravine-like streets, while entire families, tortured by heat, crouch on the few balconies and rusted fire escapes to seek the relief of a vagrant breeze. In this Manhattan where green areas are at a premium, a spacious terrain along the rivers has been retrieved. There rows of apartment buildings have been constructed at sharp angles to the mass of the city and with a good deal of space between them. These stand high above green lawns, with windows and balconies turned toward the sun. Of course there are now thousands of such apartment houses everywhere—buildings which have been built with consideration of light and weather conditions and then surrounded by greenery. But that it was possible to build such a project on the incredibly expensive and overcrowded grounds of the world's biggest city is not only an achievement but a promise that the cities of the future must and will be different and better.

Lost ground will have to be recovered inch by inch. For example, in the course of the nineteenth century industry and commerce took a firm foothold along the rivers and waterfronts of many cities. The waters were polluted, the city population deprived of recreational facilities, and the potential beauty of the city destroyed. Chicago's lake front and San Francisco's bay area, with their considerable potential for municipal development, suffered from such an uncontrolled growth of industry. A change is slowly taking place. Chicago, a city of depressing ugliness, is now learning to exploit its natural opportunities and to create a new life center in parks along the lake as well as in the university quarter and the groups of buildings comprising the Illinois Institute of Technology (built by Mies van der Rohe).[7]

In its search for more room, industry has moved into the countryside, and commercial plants now provide an opportunity for the collaboration of architecture and landscape which a hundred years ago would have seemed a dream to the first British advocates of reform in industrial architecture. One of the finest examples of such a collaboration is the Connecticut General Insurance Company in Bloomfield, Connecticut, built by Skidmore-Owings and Merrill (1955-57). The similarity between such commercial buildings and the University Cities is particularly obvious when we look at the General Motors Technical Center in Warren, Michigan (1950-56). This group of twenty-five buildings arranged around a lake, is the work of Eero Saarinen and one of the finest industrial creations of our century. The idea of technology is epitomized in the large, sometimes brightly colored wall surfaces, in the use of standard prefabricated five-foot modules throughout, and in the reduction of matter to a minimum.

The economic, as well as the ideological, principle of technology has had a profound influence on architecture. This subject, neglected by economic historians, has been treated by Sigfried Giedion in *Mechanization Takes Command* (New York, 1948). Electrification, assembly-line production, increased specialization and division of labor, and the complete elimination of handicrafts have extensively modified working-area requirements. We are faced with a paradox: working conditions and working areas have become incomparably healthier and more beautiful than they were before 1920, yet the human contribution invested in manual labor has become less and less significant.

Another example of the efforts to relieve urban congestion are the oval-shaped suburban settlements which have sprung up around large cities within the past forty years. Together with the big thoroughfares, upon which their existence depends, they create a new image of the countryside—a radiating network of buildings, with an industrial and commercial center and a residential periphery. Individual homes are separated by surrounding lawns but united by their placement and their architectural conformity. "As the basic cellular unit of the larger unit, the street, the dwelling-house represents a typical group-organism."[8]

Country and city are no longer sharply differentiated from one another, as they were in the nineteenth century. The place of employment may be as far as ten to fifty miles away from home. Every morning the city receives the workers who leave again in the evening to return to their families' semirural existence in the suburbs. As a result of this decongestion and decentralization of the metropolis, the residence problem has given way in urgency and importance to the street and traffic problem.

The highway

With its direct access and detour routes, the highway has become the "assembly line" of the landscape. Although highway construction cannot be said to have beautified the earth, it has developed as a science on a scale never known before. What seems at first to be a brutal encroachment on nature often turns out to give a cinematic continuity to the landscape. The Roman roads that unified the European scene were hardly more radical than the modern freeway in creating new contexts of country and city. The street is as much a part of the new municipal architecture as the stairway is part of the house. But the metropolis is plagued by traffic jams which can extend for miles and make a mockery of the idea of rapid transit. Leonardo had a premonition of this problem when he designed double-level streets: one for pedestrians, the other for horses and carriages.

Within the cities there is the danger that overpopulation will ruin the finest designs of the ninetenth or early twentieth centuries. The saddest example of this is Rio de Janeiro's unique Copacabana beach, which has recently been marred by rows of skyscrapers whose backs are turned to the ocean because the beach itself is already built up. The problems of planning for human residence have become so complex that no one architect can or should be entrusted with their solution. Rather, the architect, the city planner, the traffic engineer, and the social worker have to collaborate on this monumental task.

The best thing that can result from such a situation is the creation of an environment that will combine aspects of city and country, taking into account both biological necessities and aesthetic standards.

The single house

If the city mirrors its economic, social, and spiritual components, its reflection is also determined by their representative: the individual, whose residence expresses the living standards as well as the values of a community.

European cities were once surrounded by walls, and citizens lived within their protection. Since space was limited, construction had to take an upward direction, and people became accustomed to living in several-storied, vertically arranged quarters. This custom, together with the high price of real estate, made life in an apartment house appear natural, even desirable, for the majority of the urban population. In America, however, the case is quite different, for American cities have never been enclosed by walls. Therefore, the idea of the apartment house has never taken as firm a hold on the American imagination. One exception is Manhattan, which is, after all, limited by its river boundaries. Otherwise, Americans prefer the individual home— even if it be only a one-room cabin—to an apartment. They like to live within their own walls, even if every piece of furniture and every household article has to be paid for on the installment plan. Of course, this preference for individual homes requires a large building area and also makes necessary highways and shopping centers. In other words, it poses technical problems, each of which must be solved individually. What concerns us here is the human—that is to say, the cultural—aspect of the problem. The desire to own one's own home rests on a wish to be independent and to regard the family as a discrete unity sheltered by a home. These are desirable traits not only from the point of view of the individual but also from the point of view of the state as a community of free citizens. In the early 1920's, in the "socialist" phase of architecture (now a thing of the past), long rows of houses were built in Europe by Oud, Taut, and Gropius. Although lined by lawns, they stood wall to wall, constituting an implicit but enthusiastic affirmation of the masses over the individual. However, as early as 1930, Gropius proposed a combination of small houses and skyscrapers, with the possible elimination of the medium-sized buildings, a new emphasis on available lawn area, and more space between buildings.

Where, as in Sweden, apartment houses are still considered desirable for ideological or practical reasons, they are scattered in loose patterns across the landscape, so that they lose their tenement character and look almost romantic as they jut out of their green surroundings. An indication of future developments may be found in Vällingsby, a suburb of Stockholm. There trucks are restricted to subterranean access roads and private vehicles may be driven only to the edge of town. Thus, the town's shopping and the residential centers are entirely reserved for pedestrians. The community house of Hässelby, which is inhabited by about three hundred and fifty married couples, includes stores and nursery school and a restaurant from which fully prepared meals may be ordered and brought to the apartment. It would seem that in this community work and leisure have been blended into a new rhythm that presages a future way of life. Axis and square, the basic features of the old municipal architecture, are replaced by a free play of space and solids, of natural and man-made structures. Simple geometric order and stylization give way to a freer, more complex, and more variable organization.

Wherever the architectural relationship of homes becomes freer and more variable, there is created an opportunity to improve and to make more constructive the relationship of man to man. As a result of century-old municipal subdivisions, the boroughs of contemporary London still function as active, self-governing communities. In America, the neighborhood may act as a separate community through its own P.T.A., nursery schools, and social activities. The more such organisms flourish, the greater will be the possibilities for democratic self-realization. Where the tenement-like apartment house disappears, chauvinism and communism lose their most fertile ground for growth.

But precisely because the home is an organic source of life, the uses of prefabricated houses (which can be produced assembly-line fashion by few hands in little time) are circumscribed. What such homes lack is a practical and aesthetic relationship to specific surroundings.

The "loosening up" of architecture

So far we have only spoken of the "loosening up" of the city as a whole, yet the same tendency can be observed in the individual building. Again, various forces play a part in the phenomenon. Not so much the exterior as the interior of the modern building shows the effect of the new trend. Economic reasons as well as social considerations have caused the disappearance of partition walls, so that now architecture demonstrates and promotes the interdependence and interlocking of home life and work. Light and air make their appearance, together with a pattern of freely arranged spatial cubes. In office buildings and banks, rows of desks and machines form a new kind of assembly line, while in residential buildings the various functions of home life achieve new integration. However, opportunities for peace, introspection, and quiet are often neglected in favor of assuring the flexibility of family life. Both home life and work activity take on an extrovert quality heightened by the fact that nature itself is drawn into the service of the building. The glass windows, which now cover at least one wall of the structure, allow light to flood the interior and direct the eye outward to the landscape. Dürer might not have produced his engraving of St. Jerome in his cell without the "inner light" which appears through the bottled glass window panes of a secluded study. And who knows what would have happened to Schopenhauer's philosophy of pessimism in a glass-encased living room opening upon a sunny terrace?

Water, as well as light, may be allowed to enter the modern building: swimming pools may be separated from the rest of the house only by a glass wall; and Frank Lloyd Wright erected the Kaufmann house, "Falling Water" (Coonesville, Pennsylvania, 1936-37), above a waterfall. However, this aesthetic Rousseauism, this "back to nature" feeling, too, has its limits, for organic nature continues with its own processes, which include noise, insects, mold, and decay.

The happiest results of this new open style are to be found among such community buildings as schools, museums, and churches. In these projects, the architect is not only applying new aesthetic theories and principles of heightened functionalism, but also attempting a symbolic expression of contemporary ideas on education, culture, and religion.

Religious architecture

So far we have concentrated on the practical aspects of architecture, although we have proceeded from the conviction that so-

ARCHITECTURE

called functional elements are much more dependent on the basic creative conception than is generally assumed. In church architecture, however, the function, the purpose, is (or at least ought to be) part of a larger spiritual concept. This function inspires the architect to find a symbolic expression for the concept in one of two ways: by drawing attention to the community of believers and their worship, or by emphasizing the illumination from above, demonstrating symbolically the mystery of grace. The second approach frequently leads to an expressive—if not expressionistic—heightening of style, as suggested by medieval churches. Le Corbusier's Ste. Marie du Haut in Ronchamp is of this type; what this work of architecture embodies is not the beatific light from above but the cry *de profundis* (**IX**). The roof slants inward, like a canvas cloth, over curved walls of concrete. The interior is not flooded with light; instead, dusk reigns and voices are hushed to a whisper. This type of church architecture makes possible bold expressions of piety, but pseudomysticism and architectural dilettantism as well. Through fake solemnity the church may constitute a kind of architectural anticipation of grace.

Another group of architects conceives of the church as a community house, as the *ecclesia orans*. The interior is kept simple: benches face the pulpit or altar, and only the spatial arrangement—the distribution of color, matter, and light—lend to the plain meeting room an air of concentration and dedication, of expectant readiness. Nothing is being anticipated beyond the given purpose, but that in itself is an expression of a new piety which knows that "the spirit bloweth where it listeth," and that man's part can be no more than a humble receptiveness (**X**).

Today, painting, stained glass, sculpture, and tapestry are all incorporated into church architecture as a matter of course. An excellent example of such an all-embracing art is the chapel designed by the agnostic Henri Matisse in gratitude for the nuns of Vence, who had nursed him. Every detail of this chapel, down to the priest's vestments, bears the stamp of Matisse's style.

X. Saarinen, altar: MIT Chapel (1955), Cambridge, Massachusetts

Although, to some, the chapel may seem somewhat reminiscent of a fashion salon, the fact remains that it is an honest and fully realized affirmation of faith in the created world, in man, and in the Christian tradition of which the artist feels himself a part. In some ways our age resembles the Baroque Age, when the two aspects of religion—faith and grace—took their bread from the world and their wine from the heavens.

It is not necessarily an architecture dedicated to religion that expresses man's highest aspirations. The image of man may find a pure and fully realized interpretation in any building designed for community use—and religious art itself can do no more. Therefore not only churches but also schools, museums and other community buildings offer material for examining contemporary aesthetics within the context of modern existence.

The new style

Let us consider once more the character of the new style in architecture and its place in society. We have observed that architecture creates shapes in space and with space. This, in essence, means that architecture entails a new conception of what constitutes matter. A ring, for example, owes its appearance to the circle and to the void within the circle. This combination of matter and of the absence of matter leads to a reciprocal relation: on the one hand, matter becomes less heavy because free space relieves it of some of its weight and, on the other hand, matter affects the surrounding space and makes it a part of the over-all arrangement and order. Such a view of the potentialities of matter is more inspired and more dynamic than that of the nineteenth century, and it may well be that it is related to the new physics, which has given us a new philosophy of energy and matter. Modern science sees the world as composed of an infinite field of forces whose relations and combinations determine the structure of the universe as well as that of the atom. Today, architecture offers a parallel interpretation of such functions, whether it be the house in the landscape, the church on the square or the bridge over the river. Instead of hiding its functions, modern architecture reveals them, makes use of them, and relates them to other elements.

The basic tendency of the new architecture is to give shape and definition to space. Space encloses and is, in turn, enclosed by solid matter. The architectural work is a product of the combination of the shape of space and the shape of matter. This new conception of form in terms of relations is no longer bound to Euclidean geometry. As the new mathematics goes beyond Greek and Arabic mathematics, so the new architecture—no longer focused on delimited bodies but on the curve of the parabola—vaults all enclosures and describes the leap of energy into infinite space. Proportion is still a valid concept of the new architecture (Le Corbusier has written a whole book about the "module"), but the proportions in question are not predetermined by the human body. Instead they are developed out of given, variable relations; hence the surprise element in so many contemporary buildings. Also, the new building materials— chiefly steel, glass, and concrete—lead to new forms of expression; conversely, the desire for new modes of expression may give rise to the development of new materials, such as plastics. Apart from the technical interest inherent in the concrete and steel skeleton, there is also the urge to make the materials known as such—the wish to display them as materials and to develop their boldest possibilities.

Thanks to these new building materials, the architectural body may overcome the laws of gravity: it may hang or float and ignore the ground. Every constituent part of a building may now be composed of voids and solids. Gropius has spoken of the "growing preponderance of voids over solids"[9] in connection with the use of materials that allow the air to enter. And, finally, thanks to glass and glass-like materials, the exterior and the interior interpenetrate and the building becomes open and transparent, in accordance with modern man's inexhaustible thirst for space and light and his flight from all that is heavy and opaque. The wall is no longer meant to separate and lock out; instead, it has become a "membrane." The scope of expression is now without limit.

Light, airiness, looseness—these ideals of mobile contemporary man are also expressed in the generous layout of communities and streets, schools and museums. Planning and spaciousness have assumed a completely new relationship to one another and have caused a considerable change in the surface view of the earth.

But there is also a delimiting aspect to the new architecture—one connected with the image of man it creates and the kind of space it allows him. What the contemporary building lacks is a spiritual expression of power. Since we no longer accept power as a divine trait or hereditary right, architecture no longer symbolizes claims of authority. Where power does exist, as in government buildings and structures designed for economic and social corporations, it seems mostly to have been dissected into its many component functions. The corporate will is frequently veiled behind a cellular division of labor. The architecture of fascist and communist states, which indeed does express a concentration of power, reveals at the same time either its ideological emptiness or its dependence on older conceptions no longer valid.

The opposite camp, that of the individualists, is also subject to limitation and error. Here the room, the chamber as a cell enclosed by four walls, is rejected on the grounds that it is too rigid an entity. Group functions trespass upon the private life of the individual and rob him of his potential for peace, concentration, and solitude. In the modern home, it is the extrovert outlook that triumphs. If history moved in a straight line of evolution instead of zigzagging between action and reaction, there might be reason for alarm at this architectural symbolism. But prophecies concerning the historical progression of mankind necessarily take a short view. One thing, however, is certain: even if the only surviving record of mankind were to be its architecture, it would be clear that the twentieth century marks a new phase of man's evolution.

SCULPTURE

We have seen that modern architectural works are to be understood basically as plastic shapes in space. According to such a
definition, architecture's closest relative in the arts is sculpture.
Both use space as an essential element, as is evident from the
fact that modern sculpture is frequently, and by preference,
exhibited and photographed in the open. The Museum of Modern
Art in New York set a standard for other contemporary museums
when it arranged its sculptures in a garden.
Henry Moore's "King and Queen" (1952-53) stands silhouetted
against the open air (**XI**), radiating its power into space and, in
turn, absorbing space into itself. Here, in the interplay of light
and shadow, the play of its own forms becomes apparent. In
standing against space, their very nature also undergoes a

change: they become more than artistic shapes. Like the stones of Stonehenge they assert the permanence of their existence. Formed by the hand of man, they stand upright against the current of time and the formless expanse of space. Set free by their creator, they declare their independent existence.

The creature in space

If we accept the thesis that modern sculpture is concerned with producing creations that have an independent existence and a nature of their own, then the difference between objective and nonobjective sculpture becomes a great deal less significant. If our main definition of a modern building is *a body in space*, then our definition of a modern sculpture must be *a creature in space*. As is appropriate to an art of shape rather than of construction, sculpture has worked its way back to its original point of departure: the work of art is recognized as a being that pits itself against the surrounding void. In contrast to the sculpture of the nineteenth century, which imitated idea or reality, the sculpture of the late nineteenth and twentieth centuries returns to the simple, original form—the *Gestalt* as such.

Until Wilhelm Lehmbruck shifted to a medieval expressiveness, the initial tendency of the new movement was to look toward classical models. In Lehmbruck's "Kneeling Woman" (1911), which is typical of all his later works, is seen an elongation of the limbs, as in the sculptures of Moissac. This expresses a principle of growth into something beyond itself; it implies an emergence from quiet self-containment. If we thus assume that the exaggeration of dimensions corresponds to an intensification of meaning, then we are justified in asking what that meaning is. The answer is found in the gesture of the woman. The hand over her breast suggests self-protection as well as humility: a created being unfolds in the light of the divine spirit.

The spirit of Expressionism blended harmoniously with the artist's personality and sculptural task when Ernst Barlach peopled the empty niches in the façade of the Gothic church of St. Catherine in Lübeck with his figures (1930-33; **XII**). (The last of these figures were designed after World War II by Gerhard Marcks.) Barlach's cripple and his singing girl, typifying fundamental aspects of human sorrow and joy, respectively, submit to a divine law of life. Matter constitutes the impenetrable kernel of Barlach's sculpture. Where Lehmbruck eases the burden of weight, Barlach concentrates and condenses it. Space remains a force outside his figures—a threatening force, alien and unreachable, that plays the role of fate; man is rebellious and revolts against it, he is powerless and it destroys him, he entrusts himself to it and it carries him.

A content so specific and determined is rare in twentieth-century sculpture and peculiar to the sculptor-poet Barlach. His concern with subject matter might occasionally have been burdensome to the formal aspects of his work had they not been saved by the intuition of the genuine sculptor. Even so, his art has its weaknesses and limitations of form. He builds up the bodies of his figures by separating the individual surface planes with sharp, pointed lines and edges that look as if they had been carved with a knife. Very likely he derived this technique from woodcarving for it is not a quality inherent in sculpture but, rather, a mannerism he forced upon it. In a most literal sense, Barlach chops off the ebb and flow of sculptural forms, the outward pressures from their own inner core and superimposes a form and a formula of expression. Fortunately he was a master of his formula and knew how to vary it superbly as well as how to blend it with his respective content.

The humanist position

Masters who are praised in their own time are those innovators in whose work the invisible spirit of an age assumes concrete shape.

We contemporaries have no way of knowing which innovations will prove fertile and which will not. Therefore historical justice requires us to look also at the work of those artists who either consciously reject the new or who instinctively feel more comfortable with the traditional. Such artists can say with Chesterton: "It is only the smaller poet who sees the poetry of revolt, of isolation, of disagreement; the larger poet sees the poetry of the great agreements which constitute the romantic achievement of civilization."[10]

To perpetuate a tradition, however, the artist need not draw only upon specific traditional forms. He may also draw upon the general humanistic awareness of the West. A powerful cultural current flows from Phidias through Michelangelo to Keats's "Ode on a Grecian Urn" and throughout its course the human figure is seen as the apogee of perfection. One reason why this humanistic tradition is so strong is the enormous influence of Greek art. From the height of their position as initiators, the Greeks were able to cast their shadow over what followed. In Reims, Naumburg, and Florence the human image reached other forms of perfection, but these carved images did not become such substantial parts of our tradition because their makers did not stand at the beginning of European creative life. From god to satyr, Greek art went so far in identifying artistic appearance with the human figure that for two thousand years the sculptural imagination of the West was focused on the human shape. Thus, until the advent of contemporary art, humanism became a kind of second nature. It is this instinctive humanism which the sculptors of the "middle" position are defending.

Carl Milles, the great modern creator of fountains, is the Nordic story teller of the classical tradition. His supple bronze bodies do not themselves contain great plastic power of expression, but in their context—surrounded by air and water—they display

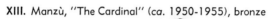

XIII. Manzù, "The Cardinal" (ca. 1950-1955), bronze

SCULPTURE

the mobility and joyousness of Ariel. His fountains have added to the beauty of cities from Stockholm to St. Louis.

Giacomo Manzù's sculptures also stand outside the main stream of contemporary art (XIII). They assert themselves by means of a language all their own. His figures—whether that of a cardinal or that of a young swimming or dancing girl—always have an element of smiling irony which seems to deprive matter of its claim to gravity. Manzù likes to use the cloak as a broad sculptural plane, and he seems to suggest that the human body itself is something like a cloak. There is a transitory quality about his figures, as if they are on the verge of shedding their identity as one sheds a piece of clothing.

From Cubism to abstraction

Cubism, and with it Cubist sculpture, postulated that the anatomically conditioned body had to be geometrically organized if the regeneration of plastic shapes was to be achieved. The movement started with the once highly promising sculptures of Archipenko and dramatically ended with Zadkine's manneristic "Memorial for the Destruction of Rotterdam" (1953-54). Many artists were concerned with the application of the aesthetic theories of Cubism to sculpture. Yet Cubist painting made bolder innovations when it created space out of interpenetrating and overlapping planes than Cubist sculpture could do, when it re-styled the organic body and reduced it to geometric—or, rather, to geometricizing—forms. Accordingly, the most significant Cubist sculptors are those who outgrew Cubism: Picasso, Julio Gonzales, and Henri Laurens. Working in close cooperation, Picasso and Gonzales discovered between 1930 and 1932 a means of expression which Picasso had previously developed in his magical horror paintings of the 1920's. Some of Picasso's own paintings and drawings look as if they had been conceived as sculptures and then translated into pictorial values. Bones, breast, and hair become absolutes. These totally new shapes—biological metamorphoses between nature and pure form—seem animated by a current of sexuality. Yet they express not so much erotic pleasure as the threat of the blind life force experienced as shock and terror.

This is the point of departure for Gonzales' iron sculptures. The hardness of his material is in itself anticlassical: he gives us polished surfaces and curved edges, hollow spaces instead of a swelling inner form. Nails and thinner metal strips are welded on the surface to emphasize the main contours. The artist, in adding and subtracting material, expresses abstract concepts in terms that surpass anything possible in nature. With his formally lucid biological abstractions, Gonzales became one of the founders of abstract sculpture which, unlike abstract painting, remains tied to biology. That is to say, sculpture still concerns itself with the human body.

Henri Laurens eventually found his way from Cubism to a more congenial style—one of swelling, modulated forms. In the titles of his bronze works, such as "Siren" or "The Great Amphion," as well as in his illustrations, we find the continued survival of classical myths. For more than two thousand years, these myths have added both a spiritual and a sensual element to art. They remain a current flowing from the Mediterranean into the work of Laurens and of Auguste Maillol, both of whom were, in this sense, intuitively Mediterranean. Although Maillol's nymphs speak out of wider structural contexts than a mere imitation of anatomical organisms would permit, he was perhaps the last artist whose shapes present a sane, unbroken whole.

Current themes: terror and anxiety

The presentation of *mens sana in corpore sano* has ceased to be a chief concern of our time. Anxiety and terror, main themes of the twentieth century, are making their claims on sculpture.

The pre-Columbian sculpture of Mexico, which is dominated by themes of awe, fear, and terror, has stimulated the work of Henry Moore—and not merely in the sphere of technique. Like Picasso, Moore—with the instinct of a prophetic interpreter of his age—reveals the decay and destruction of the human form under natural and human forces as both a biological and a historical phenomenon. Opposed to these destructive forces are the formative elements of nature. These become conscious and take shape in and through the artist, their plastic scope extending from the larva to the skeleton. For as the larva tends toward an increase of cells and a swelling of organic matter, so the skeleton tends toward reduction, allowing empty space to penetrate the basic structure of life. These are the themes underlying the many-faceted art of Henry Moore; they give his work its unity of form and content. To be sure, when he hollows out his figures, he is primarily solving a problem of form by creating a combination of voids and solids which together provide shape—a shape that will appear in the core as well as at the surface of the sculpture. But beyond their formal meaning, these creations also express the sculptor's view of life. Existence, they seem to say, occurs between chasms of destruction.

It is from such chasms that Marino Marini's horse-and-rider groups shy away (**XIV**). Narrowly limited in his subject matter, Marini reinterprets the sepulchral sculpture of the T'ang period, yet far from the original intentions of the funeral figures of ancient China.

But more terrible than a screaming art is one of speechless fear, as we see it in the figures of Alberto Giacometti (**XV**). Bodily existence is reduced to a minimum in his needle-thin bronze figures, often no larger than the palm of a hand. These small naked human beings can be arranged like tin soldiers. Their creator has endowed them with neither an expression of action nor of feeling. The vegetative principle has no part in them, nor does

animality, nor do the moving forces of mind and spirit. They stand and they walk; homeless, they live in no-man's land. As if reflected by a distorting mirror, they are thinned-out matter that rises upward, encased by the void that faces them. These figures seem to cross de Chirico's empty squares, where the station clock points forever to the noon hour, where the smoking locomotive will never leave the station, where the shadow drawn with knifelike precision will never dissolve. The spirit of *pittura metafisica* also applies to Giacometti's sculptures, but the metaphysical situation they express is quite specifically that of a cosmic anxiety, the experience of being lost in infinite nothingness. Pascal's diary entry also applies to them: "The silence of the infinite spaces fills me with terror."

Such sculpture permits us to discern form as an agent in a minimum of matter. A similar effect is to be found in the small sculptures of the Etruscans and the Sardinians, which are also characterized by radical elongation but which lack Giacometti's sensitive modelling of surfaces. With amazement we recognize the tangibility of matter developed on almost no matter at all. There remains a question: Does the pathological nature of the compulsive idea behind the work limit the truth of its aesthetic statement? However, pathological exaltation—represented in literature by Dostoevsky or Kafka—is capable of making valid statements precisely by virtue of its obsessional single-mindedness. This is also true of Giacometti. His absurd art seems to signal the same retreat to ultimate positions found in the existential philosophy of Sartre and Heidegger. Movingly, these nudes seem to say "I am," and this *I am* is the first step toward self-recognition.

The shape

But today the act of self-recognition, inherent in the creative process, takes place not so much in the human figure as in shaped objects. The term *shaped objects*, is somewhat general but it is closer to the nature of plastic art than, say, the phrase *nonobjective sculpture*. Although contemporary sculpture does not imitate or represent nature, it creates shapes to be experienced as concrete and tangible. Titles such as "Swan" or "Chorus" indicate that the connection with nature has not been entirely disrupted. This is why the painter and ceramicist Miró rejected the designation *abstract* for his art. "Everything," he states, "is derived from the visible world. The concrete object claims my attention more and more, if only as a point of departure. There is nothing abstract in my paintings."[11] Whether these creations are also able to communicate emotions and ideas, or at least evoke associations of this kind, depends only in part on the original intent of the sculptor. The final product results from a confluence of the artistic will and a sympathetic understanding of the possibilities inherent in the forms and materials themselves. The world of shapes opens under his hands and guides him, even as it is guided by him.

Chance, idea, material, and creative power

Contemporary sculpture and painting allow more room for chance than the art of any preceding period. This statement seems to imply an abdication of the artist's will and, perhaps, of his rational faculties in the process of artistic creation. But control by reason can in fact recede once the working materials are no longer used to create a likeness of the visible world—when, instead, the materials are permitted an existence of their own and used as a point of reference for the inner images or feelings of the artist. Much of contemporary art is an art of discovery. The forms inherent in the artistic materials suggest certain concepts to the artist which he, in turn, applies to the material, forcing and molding it accordingly. The artistic achievement and its level of quality lie in the artist's attention to this give-and-take-and-give-again—in the artist's mastery of this reciprocity of chance, idea, material, and creative power.

Such a process, in which the material suggests the possibilities of the finished work to the artist is not new. It has always existed in wood-carving, for instance, where the natural shape of a piece of wood, guided by the carver, assumes the form of a sea shell, a bird, or a human face. The contemporary artist no longer relies on the visible world; instead, he heeds the suggestions of the working material in his hands as he works to produce a tangible object, a shaped thing. Only in thus transcending nature can he realize the full potential of shape and give it a free and objective development. The shaped thing may hang, float, rest lightly, or press down massively; it may turn, circle, or spin; it may receive its shape from the interplay of matter and void; it may surge in density or it may be hollow; it may be highly polished or have a truncated, corroded, bumpy, mutilated surface. *Mutilated* indicates that the treatment and shaping of inorganic matter contain associations with the world of psychic and mental experiences. Damaged material evokes thoughts of pain, suffering, and human injury.

The dissociation from nature

Everything that sculpture has to say can be stated in terms of what is perceptually familiar as well as in terms that do not relate to reality. Doubtless, the possibilities for experimentation with form are greater in nonobjective art, but this increased freedom carries with it the danger of developing into a playful, irresponsible, purely accidental, or purely private art. Furthermore, we must also consider the demands made on the spectator. To absorb a complex of forms that has never existed before calls for a high degree of sympathetic understanding, usually involving repeated viewings of the work, perhaps even over a period of time. Beyond this difficulty, there is a cultural problem: such a work of art relinquishes its place in the world of universal experience when it ceases to refer to the visible world and speaks only of itself and of its creator. When we visit a contemporary exhibition, we are no longer moving among representations, but among mere patterns, more rarely among truly shaped objects and still less frequently among genuine creations. Art is therefore exposed to the danger of fragmentation into private worlds. Until now, visible reality provided a means of communication between artist and spectator. Every civilization is based on such communication, for without it there can be no such thing as a living community. In all cultures, sculpture has always been primarily concerned with the human figure and it was in the human figure that daemonic, magical, and religious concepts materialized. It was in the animated human figure that the Greeks discovered the realm of beauty. It was in the human figure that the laws of sculpture itself became manifest, laws governing the demonstration of mass in planes and depth, the visual manifestation of weight and proportion. But the development of a mode of expression that was pertinent only to sculpture already contained the possibility of a transition from an art that represented nature to one that formed shaped objects. Thus the advent of modern sculpture did not constitute a breach with the past, but rather a continuation of a trend toward new fields of application and wider possibilities of expression. The advent of modern sculpture began around 1910 —almost simultaneously with that of abstract painting—in the work of the Rumanian-born sculptor Brancusi. It is not an accident that it occurred in Paris, for it was in Paris that the greatest understanding of the autonomy of artistic expression had developed and it was there that Cézanne's absolute style of painting had found its first fervent disciples.

Geometric and morphological shapes

Since 1910 the sculpture of shapes (as we shall call it, having decided that it is neither abstract nor nonobjective), has taken two main directions: one is an art of geometric forms related to

Cubism; the other, a morphological art which, in analogy to nature itself, produces an endless variety of beings. It is the morphological sculpture that begins with Brancusi. Its scope is as limitless as the imagination of the artist and the inspiration he derives from his materials. Fundamentally, it is impossible to describe these shapes since creations of this sort have, after all, no existence outside art. One can attempt to describe the individual phenomenon, but we must bear in mind that the essentials —the shaped context, the nexus of form—cannot be adequately demonstrated by verbal analogies. In the sculpture of Brancusi there are no expressive distortions or intensifications of reality. Instead, Brancusi animates the working material itself, thus increasing its inherent expressiveness. The shape entitled "Leda" (**XVI**) is a hollow body of metal, smoothly polished to a constantly changing shimmer. From a narrow base, it curves outward and upward on both sides and, like the flame of a candle, comes to a point: rising, swelling, narrowing, always reflecting light. The title is not even necessary to evoke the associations that give this shape, in analogy to nature, the appearance of being slender and elegantly feminine. Many of Brancusi's figures convey the impression of strength relieved by a note of playfulness. He seems to take us into a world of primary conditions where form comes to life and stirs for the first time. The term *primary conditions* calls for a comment. The experience of initial situations, of origins, fascinates Henry Moore, dominates Brancusi's work, and concerns many contemporary sculptors. The artist penetrates hitherto untouched stone and wood. The object he creates is a being which has not yet pre-empted the artist's task by achieving a highly developed form of its own. The more amorphous and primary the original mass, the more dramatic the artist's encroachment will appear.

The primary conditions of matter
In the sculpture of Jean Arp the shaping power of nature seems

to emerge before our eyes from a kind of protoplasm. The sensory empathy that enables us to feel that the curve of a hill or the swelling of a sail is beautiful and meaningful is here brought to bear on the material. Plastic movement comes sensuously alive and, in the process, dead matter assumes visual expressiveness. Such sculpture exists in the presence of organic wellsprings; it draws upon the primary facts of birth and death, removed from the complexities of a fully flowering civilization. Hence it seems related to primitive art: both carry suggestions of the numb, the undeveloped. One may even go so far as to say that the idea of ripeness and perfection as an aim, as the end product in a line of development, runs counter to today's creative processes. The idea of perfection has, as it were, retreated into the creative process itself, and that process reveals only gradually to the creator what direction his work is taking. Since nature no longer provides the model, perfection has ceased to be the final goal, but must instead be sought in individual stations *along* the way.

The value of decay

The sculptor is inspired not only by primary forces but also by the environment to which matter is exposed. He reacts with the highest sensitivity to texture, and the essence of matter is to be found in what is mossy, rusty, chapped, choppy, corroded, eroded, burst, banged, damaged. The painters and photographers of our day have joined in this voyage of discovery into the world of decay, and a new microcosm of mutilated surfaces has sprung up. Although this reflects a heightened sensitivity of the visual and tactile senses, such an explanation does not reveal the significance of these experiences. There have been artists in former times who had a special sense for such states of matter: Grünewald who, like the modern artist, treated corrosion not only because it had an aesthetically provocative effect but also because it interpreted the reality of decomposition. Decomposition is the aesthetic equivalent for the experience of isolation, the threat of matter, and the destruction of causal relations. This phenomenon appears in literature, too, shortly before, during, and after World War I (for example, in Kafka's description of a wound in his story *A Country Doctor*).

This new sense for the aesthetic value of decaying or mutilated materials has led sculptors to use a highly effective tool, the blow torch, which causes partial erosion. This technique can imbue metal with the appearance of old ship sides, anchors, or barbed wire entanglements, and facilitates the suggestion of such shapes as aggressive crustaceans, thorny underbrush, tangled creepers, or intertwined bodies. When Germaine Richier, Theodore Roszak (**XVII**), Seymour Lipton, or Reg Butler (**XVIII**) speak through such shapes, they show us creatures of fear, of paralysis, of terror. It seems natural enough that suffering man should find identifying symbols for the experiences of war and mass murder of his age.

The mutilation of the organic form

In the work of Henry Moore and Jacques Lipchitz sculpture produces specific and distinct statements. By hollowing out their figures, both sculptors arrived at what may be called an inner and an outer sculpture. The interaction of voids and shaped volumes result in greatly increased plastic mobility as well as in rich contrasts of light and shadow, adding a quality lacking in sculptures that deal in surfaces only. Yet we must not overlook the monstrous aspect of the physiological shrinkage in Moore or the doughy masses of Lipchitz. The hollowed out bodily shapes have the effect of a radical mutation of the organism, conveying once again a sense of mutilation. The significant and widespread predilection for the pre-Columbian culture of Mexico and Lipchitz's fondness for African sculpture (which he shares with many of his generation) is chiefly, but by no means exclusively, a matter

of formal interest. These artists are also attracted by the terror image with its demons, and by the archetypal image with its magical properties. Inherent in both are psychic shock effects which neither classical nor medieval sculpture could offer in the same manner. Thus, without underrating the importance of formal considerations, in the last analysis it was the desire for a heightened vitality which led, paradoxically, to the mutilation of the natural organism.

The work of art: a storehouse of vitality

Perhaps at this point we hold the key to the nature of nonobjective or semiobjective art. If we visualize the creative instinct as a river, with its source in the ego of the artist, and as its mouth or estuary the final product—the work of art—then we realize that before the twentieth century the flow of this river remained hidden. The finished product did not show the traces of experimentation and of the trial and error of the working process. Contemporary art, on the other hand, charts the river from source to sea. The work frequently exhibits the traces of all the stages it has gone through; it is an object that may still be changing and growing, not a work that has been finished. The implications are twofold. On the one hand, there is an implied mistrust toward the very possibility of completion and perfection; on the other hand, there is a fascination with the artist's functioning relationship to the thing he has shaped. Thus the work has an aesthetic and a vital value as long as it is bound by an umbilical cord to the searching ego. To be sure, the work of art is a goal, but the road that led to the goal is kept open, and the intense vitality inherent in the act of creation is preserved. The work of art offers us not only a shape but its originating vitality as well. The polish of a finished product has given way to the searching liveliness of inventing man. Expressive values do not necessarily appear on an activated surface or with a flowing silhouette. They can also be demonstrated as minimal deviations in static blocks, columns, or intact pieces of matter. Such is the sculpture of Fritz Wotruba, Isamu Noguchi, or of Louise Nevelson's wooden boxes filled with shapes. Discretion, silence, and concentrated power speak with hushed voices in these cryptic formations.

As a counterpart to biological vitality, we find an interest in mechanical relations and connections, demonstrated in functional machines that do not function. In today's exhibitions we can find all the variants of machine aesthetics; engineering principles, such as spanning, clamping, tying, and stratifying, are enjoyed for their own sake. Jean Tinguely probably went farthest in this direction, when he created his motorized "Junk Mobile," a belated Dadaism in sculpture—the antimachine made from machine parts.

Contemporary sculpture vacillates between two poles of expression: on one side the artists who express a subjective vitality; on the other, those who produce crystalline dreams of objective perfection. The latter are the alchemists of transparent bodies. Their art is the experimental laboratory for the interplay of regular and irregular shapes, where suggestions from microcosmic optics are put to use and changed into spectacular images. The awakening self-awareness of the Industrial Age gave rise to the experiments of Naum Gabo, Antoine Pevsner (**XIX**), Laszlo Moholy-Nagy, Alexander Calder (**XX**), and Richard Lippold in which a world of interpenetrating shapes, frequently transparent, parallels the architectural dreams of a Mies van der Rohe or a Frank Lloyd Wright. As soon as the concepts of Mies, Le Corbusier, and Niemeyer became actual buildings, they demonstrated the peculiar appropriateness of these light and line sculptures which were originally designed on the drawing board and constitute in effect a kind of architectural sculpture. The sculptures of Pevsner, which for decades were considered only speculative experiments, can be seen today not only in museums but also at the University

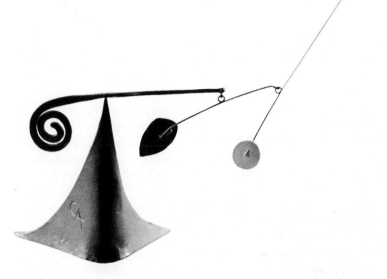

of Caracas and on the Esso building in the heart of New York. In Gabo's design for a theater and auditorium for the Palace of the Soviets (1931) we see him anticipate the suspended, curved, thin-shelled architecture of the present.[12]

In an age whose architecture has taken transparence and light beyond the practical or necessary in order to shape a new feeling of life, these sculptures, too, present the drama of light and motion, transparence, radiation, reflection, and variations of density and light as significant expressions of the age. Again, like architecture, they contain an exploration of the formal possibilities of the new materials. When we look at the movement of these shaped forms, they turn out to consist of regular, geometrically predictable progressions in space, usually spiral. The spiral fulfills a dual function, for it can demonstrate linear as well as spatial relations. In order to bring out the aesthetic interplay of a two-dimensional shape with a three-dimensional one, the artist shows us the consonance of a line moving through space. The interaction of equal progressions produces a visible, spatial rhythm which relates these works both to dance and to music. Shifting and moving through light and space, free of all individual experiences and not bound by necessity, they speak of their creator's effort to unveil the order of number and rhythm. They conjure up a weightless existence, the Icarus dreams of the technical age.

Compared to the nineteenth century, the twentieth has brought with it a new flowering of the art of sculpture. This fact alone should make us suspicious of prophecies heralding the "end" of art. Admittedly, the transition from a sculpture of the body to a sculpture of shapes has dehumanized art, but in the process sculpture gained a greater power of spontaneous invention which allows increased thematic and plastic flexibility. For the first time since the Baroque era, sculpture is again a vital art.

PAINTING

At the American art exhibition in Moscow in 1959, Peter Blume's surrealistic painting "The Eternal City" was shown. According to *Time Magazine* (August 19, 1959), the public disliked this biting dream-satire on Mussolini's Rome until an explanatory sign was hung next to it which said: "Antifascist." From then on, the painting met with approval. This episode is typical of hundreds of similar occurrences. Most people still demand of a work of art the same degree of realism that was wanted in the nineteenth century, because this demand arises from a vital and nonaesthetic instinct: the instinct for preserving and confirming existence itself. Apparently the essential dialogue set up by a work of art depends upon its allowing the spectator to identify what he sees in the painting with his own experiences and impressions. These may be aesthetically sublimated or sentimentally degraded, but in either case the spectator will find in the content of the painting an assurance that what the isolated "I" has experienced has also been encountered by another "Thou" and that the experience has been of a kind that could be formulated and recreated through the medium of art. Therein, and not in the perception of form, lies the naïve and partially misunderstood effect of the work of art. The experience of form is smuggled in under the cover of content.

Yet by the nineteenth century the artists themselves, in radical contrast to this tendency, were losing interest in reality as subject matter. Although Courbet proudly proclaimed a credo of realism in his exhibition of 1855, it is surprising how little of everyday city life the realistic painters conveyed compared to the realistic novelists. Courbet himself followed his own program only in the "Stonebreakers" and in the "Funeral of Ornans"; otherwise he generally contented himself with the tried and trusty themes of a fine craft, with still-lifes, nudes, landscapes, and portraits.

Thus, while the public was still insisting on "reality," the most advanced painters of the last century were coming to consider the role of appearances as "content" less and less significant. Since the Enlightenment, the motivating forces of the social mechanism had become increasingly apparent, and this knowledge carried with it a proportional increase of skepticism, pessimism, and adverse criticism of the created world. For the genuine artist of the nineteenth century, the bustle of human activity was probably less wonderful and astonishing a spectacle than it had been in previous centuries. In landscape painting, too, a gradual decomposition of objective, tangible nature set in. Reality became intangible, relative, something to be subjectively assimilated. Since Constable and Turner, painters have been increasingly fascinated by atmosphere but, since Courbet, they have also come to attach a new importance to an individual "handwriting" of the brush.

But in proportion to the diminishing of reality, there has been an increase of insight into the independent life of artistic expression. Guillaume Apollinaire therefore could write: "It is the social function of great poets and artists to change continuously the appearance which nature has to the human eye." [13] That is to say, the artist sees to it that reality does not appear worn and drained of meaning.

In 1905, the Paris group of painters whom the critics called *Les Fauves* ("the wild beasts") struck a blow in defense of vitality and self-expression, which they believed were in danger of becoming thin and deracinated. The group included Matisse, Dufy, Vlaminck, Derain, and Braque. At the time, their paintings seemed revolutionary with their unbroken, violent colors. Today, however, we see in them a direct coloristic continuation of Seurat's and Signac's neo-Impressionism. The same holds true of the early phase of German Expressionism, with Kirchner, Heckel, Pechstein, Schmidt-Rottluff, and Nolde, whose coloristic technique shows a development somewhat parallel to that of the French Fauvists. In both cases, nature is the point of departure, while the aim is the display of an orgiastic feeling for life. The symbolism of Redon, Munch, and the young Picasso had been drenched in a passive consciousness of the suffering world. This new consciousness turned into active revolt, but that "sequence of destructions" which, according to Picasso, forms the origin of all creation, has its constructive aspect, too. The old order is to be destroyed, and the liberated artist celebrates a revengeful triumph by means of distortions and "ugly" forms.

In the work of the painters of the *Brücke*, we can also observe this joy in destruction leading to a new beginning. When the organic human form is transformed into fetish and mask, it becomes impossible for the rational faculties to keep a check upon the content of a painting. Reason is replaced by liberated life-forces. Thus there emerges out of aggressive destructiveness, out of barbarism and primitivism, a new kind of painting—one that will replace the statement *it is* of a five-hundred-year-old naturalism with the new art of *I am*.

Picasso's *"Demoiselles d'Avignon"*

In a work of art a return to the primal forces of existence can be experienced only through form. When Expressionism and Fauvism chose irregular, grating, zigzagging designs, they were expressing the destruction of organic contexts, but they were also building a new universe with splinter forms that were far removed from nature. Continuing in the tradition of Cézanne's "Bathers," Picasso, in his *"Demoiselles d'Avignon"* (1907; New York, Museum of Modern Art; **XXI**), showed that one could construct a kind of second nature out of abstractions of original nature. We can trace this progression into new territory on the canvas itself. The left side and the middle figures, as well as the preparatory drawings, are akin to the forms of Fauvism. But the still-life, the two figures on the right, and the right side of the background show a metamorphosis of faces into masks obviously influenced by African art, and a metamorphosis of the design into sharp-edged, cubistic shapes. The left side is expressively distorted, the right side structurally altered. Nevertheless, the painting has unity. For the first time in Western art, a painting rejects the spirit of humanism and naturalism out of programmatic aggressiveness. This canvas stands at the crossroads, with an evocative power so painful that it was not until 1930 that it was reproduced in a monograph on the artist.[14]

If we compare it to another equally large painting created that year, Matisse's *"Joie de Vivre"* (Barnes Foundation, Merion, Pennsylvania), we are struck by the sense of continuity in Matisse, by the sense of revolt in Picasso. In Picasso's painting, theme and

form part company. The content offers no reason why these nude figures should have been painted or should appear in the manner in which they do appear. In the process of their development, a new principle of painting had been born: Cubism. Thus Cubism, a pre-eminently formal style with roots in Cézanne's work, makes its appearance in a painting of dramatic forcefulness, whose novel character is the result of aesthetic passion. In the revolutionary act of creation, birth and destruction are inextricably intertwined.

Expressionism

Shortly after the appearance of the Fauvists in France, Expressionism emerged in Germany, but its connection with the contemporary French movement needs to be clarified. The members of the *Brücke* in Dresden occasionally denied the connection altogether. Although the Fauvists broke through to pure color a little earlier than the Dresden group, the trend toward the graphic, the emphasis on a twisted line drawing that spans and stretches across the canvas, is of purely German origin. Color and drawing are put into the service of a dramatic intensification of the joy and pain in human experience. An impulse not only of religious fervor but also of egotistical rhetoric separated the German painters of this epoch from those of the other nations. They offered up man's suffering in the chalice of their art. Hence Germany alone produced significant religious paintings at that time. There are three distinct components to Expressionism: a North German-Saxon group centered about the artists' league "*Die Brücke*"; a South German-Russian group centered around the "*Blaue Reiter*"; and, finally, the solitary figure of Oskar Kokoschka who came from Vienna. When one considers how relatively little color had mattered in the history of German painting during the nineteenth century, then Expressionism's exaltation of color appears as an act of liberation. There is ecstasy in the oil paintings, and even more in the water colors, of Nolde (**XXII**),

Heckel and Schmidt-Rottluff. Their fervor goes beyond that of Fauvism.

Among the painters of the *Brücke*, Ernst Ludwig Kirchner is the most singular. His world ranged from the artist's garret to the meadows of the Swiss Alps. There was something feverish in his productivity: thousands of his paintings, prints, and drawings came to light in the auctions of the postwar period. Although his jagged style often conveys a mannered effect, the over-all impression is as unified and convincing as that of Nolde or Schmidt-Rottluff. In addition to the unmixed tube colors, the greens, yellows, and reds of the other Expressionists, he uses such colors as a fashionable violet and an exotic yellow; his artistic personality is the richer and the more complex for this coloristic expansion. In Kirchner's art are contained the basic components of Expressionism, with its mixture of urban intoxication and the search for God, of eroticism and natural purity. In one field, that of wood cuts, Kirchner's achievement is overwhelming and completely original. Wood cutting is the most direct of all graphic forms of expression, and since the days of Gauguin it has been the favorite medium of those artists who use the techniques of cutting and incision in an attempt to find their way back to a genuine experience.

Only Rouault's paintings of the Fauvist period, his inhuman prostitutes and corrupt judges, display a dramatic intensity comparable to that of the German Expressionists. In Rouault's creations, form speaks with brutal force about brutal matters. Genuine Expressionism gives us the feeling that the artist sees his work as the medium through which he can tell the truth about reality. This presupposes that he has a certainty of truth, and it is precisely this certainty which gives to Expressionism its strong ethical undertones.

The group of painters active in Munich—particularly Franz Marc and August Macke—showed a similar preoccupation, but they were more strongly influenced by France. Guided by the slightly older Kandinsky, they called their group the *Blaue Reiter*. They ultimately arrived at Cubism and absolute color because they have been born and bred to a concern with pure form.

Kokoschka's development, like Munch's, runs counter to the current of the century. He starts as an Expressionist but, toward the end of the 1920's, turned to a naturalistic-impressionistic style. The two phases are combined by the unique personality of the artist; they constitute, moreover, a meaningful psychological development from self-dramatizing subjectivity to a more objectively observant attitude. Inspiration and improvisation give his work the air of something still unfinished, suggesting a process rather than an end product. With the exception of the Dresden pictures, with their broad tapestry effects, Kokoschka's early work allows reality to emerge as a spiritualistic plasma, whereas in maturity he developed an open system of colors and lines. With Kokoschka, we participate in a genesis of insight and its translation into form. Expressionism represents the last stage of Zola's definition of art as "nature seen through a temperament." Nature still exists as one side of the scale, but the weights have all been shifted to the other side, that of temperament. With Cubism, Zola's formula loses its validity altogether.

Matisse, who belongs to late Impressionism and Fauvism, also is basically an Expressionist. The emotional power of this artist arises from his ability to combine visual elements which normally appear disparate. Thus, where we expect a spatial succession we find instead colored planes next to one another, creating linear designs by their juncture. Line, color and plane become elements of a shaped design which is intended to be decorative beyond all else. That art could, among other things, be ornamental, is something that had frequently been forgotten since the advent of naturalism. But with Matisse, art becomes ornamental again, as it had been in the eighteenth century. At the same time, his pictures seem to demonstrate how much power of expression can lie in a line or in a colored surface. It is this last aspect of his work that makes of Matisse a pioneer of abstract painting. Otherwise, his art still professes the credo of the nineteenth century; for, in the last analysis, his joy in life aims at "beauty"—that is, at sensuous charm.

Cubism

Cubism came into being as a reaction to the freely decorative and uncontrolled elements of Fauvism. Although its immediate inspiration is to be found in the sharp-edged African carvings and the art of Cézanne, we must not overlook its relation to Pascal's "spirit of geometry," a spirit which has returned again and again to haunt the consciousness of European artist-thinkers. Geometry has been fascinating to artists because of the aesthetic satisfaction produced by rationally constructed, harmoniously proportioned figures. In a frequently quoted passage in Plato's *Philebos* (51, c-e), we read of the sensuous pleasure derived from abstract figures which are "free from the sting of desire." But such a pleasure is merely aesthetic; the deeper levels of the psyche have no part in it. Only after the neo-Platonic concept of the harmony of the spheres had made of mathematics and geometry a key to understanding the universe did it become possible to ascribe to abstract figures that intellectual and psychic content which medieval and Renaissance theologians and aestheticians discovered in them. The occasional geometric abstractions which one finds among the drawings of Leonardo and Dürer reflect such theories; they are "key" attempts at unlocking the mystery of the universe and exploring its harmonious relationships.

But the Cubist art of Picasso, Braque, and Gris is fundamentally different from such geometric experiments. It is not based on a faith in the rationality of the created world. The Cubist paintings of about 1910 are, if not hostile to meaning, at least devoid of it.

It is true that they have been freed from the "sting of desire," but they do not point beyond themselves; they are self-sufficient formal shapes. Subject matter and color, those elements which could arouse either mental or sensuous associations, have deliberately been suppressed. Still-life and individual figures serve as skeletons for the formal constructions. We can observe how, step by step, initially three-dimensional solids are reduced to planes and their organic context dissolved. Where nature gives us the impression of space, the Cubist painter gives us stratification upon a two-dimensional surface; where we expect directed movement, we are confronted with a state of transparent fluctuation. This result stems to some extent from the fact that several views of an object have been welded together. From a succession of views emerges simultaneity—what Apollinaire, borrowing a term from mathematics, called the "fourth dimension." In moving around the object, we gain an insight into the genesis and structure of our image of reality. Or, as Bergson says in his *Introduction to Metaphysics*: "In its eternally unsatisfied desire to embrace the object around which it is compelled to turn, analysis multiplies without end the number of points of view in order to complete its always imperfect translation." [15]

Cubism therefore represents an attempt to weld together the methods of seeing and the objects of vision into a visual order. From the revolutionary destruction of form it passes on to passionless, subtly demonstrated constructions.

In such pure construction, in what Apollinaire called *Peinture pure*, the painting itself is the object of the painting. In the words of two painter-theoreticians: "The painting is its own justification, its own *raison d'être* . . . it is an organism." And the first rejection of the word *abstract*: "In our work we are concerned neither with description nor with abstractions, but with a concrete, newly created reality." [16]

When the relationship to a reality outside the painting disappears, the model provided by nature also dissolves. That model, which had still determined the work of Cézanne and Matisse, is based on an impression already organized by consciousness. The work of art, in the process of being perfected, moves *toward* such a model. In Cubist art, for the first time in Western painting, this guiding model disappears. With the painting no longer conditioned by objects (or, at least, with the influence of objects reduced to a minimum), Juan Gris wrote: "Until the work is completed, the painter must remain ignorant of its appearance as a whole." [17] Indeed, the painter cannot know and ought not to know that final appearance, since the painting does not refer to an already existing shape but to a shape that is taking form under his hands. Only with the last stroke of his brush does it come into being. The natural image and the imagined form overlap in a state of permanent oscillation. In the very transparence of its glazes, Cubism is the painted expression of such a state.

Although the formal element is definitely dominant in the work of Picasso and the Paris Cubists, the discovery that the work of art has a reality of its own opened a vista onto the *surréalité* of the artistic shape. Juan Gris called the discovery that Cubist creation followed laws of its own, its "synthetic" phase, to distinguish it from the first, or "analytic," phase. When Picasso introduced a piece of oil cloth and a fragment of a cane chair into one of his still-lifes of 1911-12, when he wrote the letters *JOU* into it and framed the oval painting with a rope, he was chiefly composing with form and texture. Yet, in this, the earliest of his collages, he nevertheless created a work that points in the direction of the *objet trouvé*. "Objet trouvé" is—as the surrealists called it—a work in which a haphazard conglomeration of objects, such as strips of paper, matches, postage stamps, resulted in a new configuration. With the wood construction "*Mandolin*" of 1914, Picasso very decidedly leads Cubism toward the freely imagined shapes of the surrealists. Thus, the art of Cubism, although curbed by geometry, points toward an art of the imagination that will be free from the limitations of reason. Nobody has mastered this art of the imagination with greater virtuosity than Picasso himself.

Expressionist Cubism

Compared to the Cubism of Picasso, Braque, and Gris, the art of Delaunay, Léger, Chagall, Marc, and Feininger is more tradition-bound. Their work inclines towards geometry but maintains the model from nature. Such a statement must not be construed as a value judgment, for the quality of paintings in this category may range all the way from dilettantism to mastery. These paintings keep in touch with the Western tradition not so much by main-taining the naturally created object as by maintaining a context of meaning between the outer and the inner world. The ecstatic words of Franz Marc apply to all the artists in this group: "I try to heighten my sensitivity for the organic rhythm of all things, I seek to empathize in a pantheistic way with the currents of blood that flow through nature. . . ." [18] Such paintings come close to music, for they use the already existing structures of geometry in their attempt to translate the rhythm of the living world into organized symbols. We are dealing here with an art of heightened expression, which belongs by nature to Expressionism. The outer world is reborn as an inner state, while the Cubist form stands for a universal law to which both the artist and his object must sub-mit. The title *Orphisme*, coined by Apollinaire and adapted by Delaunay, conjures an art of symbols—magical, musical, and abstract.

Futurism

Futurism, too, falls within the range of expressionistic Cubism. Born of the revolutionary impetus provided by Italian writer-artists, it attempts to find its own expression for the dynamic en-ergies of the contemporary world. Futurism holds up the hectic rhythm of the Machine Age against the timeless state of oscillation which we have seen at work in French Cubism. In Balla's painting, "Swifts: Paths of Movement and Dynamic Sequences" (1913; New York; Museum of Modern Art), or, on the French side, in Marcel Duchamp's "Nude Descending a Staircase" (1912; Philadelphia Museum of Art), the technique of painting approaches that of the film strip. The titles themselves indicate sequential movement, which is developed in varied vertical and horizontal rows and layers, that finally achieve, through variety in motion, the impression of a basic figure. Here, as everywhere else in Cubism, we arrive at the principle of stratification, because matter loses its opaqueness and becomes transparent.

"Who can still believe in the opacity of bodies?" Marinetti wrote in 1910,[19] and in so asking gave for the first time conscious expression to the idea that contemporary technology tends to create an aesthetics of its own. We have already observed that modern architecture uses glass walls that allow light to penetrate the interiors, and we have spoken of the invention of new transparent materials. In painting the same principle appears with the advent of Cubism and Futurism. The old alchemists' dream of the transmutation of matter has come true in modern natural science, and its aesthetic equivalent is embodied in the plastic arts. Transparence permits the simultaneous presentation of several views or states of an object, which we have come to see as sequences. Part of the Futurist program is simultaneity, exemplified by a painting by Umberto Boccioni called "Noise of the Street Penetrates the House" (1911; *Landesgalerie*, Hanover). The unity and instantaneousness of the painting are meant to create an effect which music and poetry can achieve only within a time sequence. Interior and exterior, the surroundings and the internal world, are to become one. What holds them together is motion, the dynamics of vitality made visible through the vibration of lines and colors. But if we compare the paintings and sculptures of the Futurists with their programs, we notice that their achievement does not measure up to their proclamation of a new style.

The literature of the period, too, tried to come to grips with the problem of simultaneity, but only James Joyce found the solution in content and form in his *Ulysses* (1922). It is remarkable that at the time when artists were dissolving the old spatial and temporal concepts, Hermann Minkowsky formulated the concept of the unity of space and time with his "fourth dimension" in 1908. Apollinaire called attention to this parallel between Cubism, Futurism, and mathematics, in his *Les Peintres cubistes* (1913). It is certain that the painters did not derive their ideas directly from the exact sciences, and we may be equally certain that the mathematicians were not influenced by Cubism. Whence, then, the strange parallelism? Since Kant, the concept of a simple given reality had been disappearing from philosophy and, with the development of chemistry during the nineteenth century, from empirical science as well. The general hollowing out of the concept of reality was further promoted by social crises. The arts interpreted what philosophy and the exact sciences had first discovered. The connecting link is to be found in a specific outlook on existence, shared by an entire generation. Whereas rhythmic sequences reveal the movement of bodies and transparence shows them within a spatial setting, the color explosions of the Futurists are charged with that dynamic and revolutionary vitality to which avant-garde Europe reacted with hectic excitement before the outbreak of World War I. These explosive color effects derive ultimately from late French naturalism, where a progressive dissection of the color spectrum produced progressively stronger vibrations. In this context particular mention should be made of Seurat, whom the Futurists themselves singled out as one of their forerunners. But in Seurat's work, color vibrations still serve to represent a given world, whereas van Gogh, Seurat's direct heir, uses them to describe dynamic states of excitement. Van Gogh's colors no longer rest on the surface, but flame and flash across it. In his work and in that of the Expressionists of the North we can discern a romantic and pantheistic sense of life, but in the work of the Futurists the same ingredients combine to glorify an impersonal Machine Age which would destroy tradition and create a new reality. For this reason its form-abstractions are no longer dependent on the basic figures of the old geometry which had been used as a skeleton by the Cubists. With full insight into this fact, Carlo Carrà writes: "We reject the right angle, which we call passionless, cube and pyramid, all static forms. . . . We want the shock of all acute angles, we want the dynamic arabesque, the slanted lines which attack the senses of the spectator like arrows falling from the sky; the whirling circle, the ellipse, the spiral, the upside-down cone—the shape of explosion; we want the polyphonic and polyrhythmic shapes which correspond to a need for inner disharmony. In our opinion, the artistic sensuousness of a painting depends on such disharmony." [20]

In this last sentence we have yet another point in the program of Futurism: the "need for inner disharmony."

"The need for inner disharmony"

This expression takes us by surprise; it seems to contradict man's natural urge for equilibrium and for the elimination of painful tensions. But when tensions are eliminated, the impetus toward liberating action and creative sublimation may disappear also. Not only for the Futurists and the Expressionists, but also from Michelangelo to Dostoevsky, there has been a "need for inner disharmony," so that the sense of affliction might turn into art. With the Futurists it became a revolutionary program, because they wanted the artist actively to contribute to the regeneration of the epoch. Mussolini's glorification of the "dangerous life" arose partially from the activistic atmosphere of Futurism, which did not follow the ideologies of Marxism but those of nationalism. Italian—that is, Mussolini's—fascism had its ideological roots in Futurism's "mysticism of action" (Benedetto Croce), and as a logical result we find the Futurist painter Marinetti in a fascist military cadre.

All twentieth century Western art is imbued with this need for inner disharmony; it stems from the isolation of the artist as an outsider in middle-class society, from the loneliness of the individual facing an infinite universe, from the depersonalization of the individual within a mechanized economy, from a "re-evaluation of values" (Nietzsche) which has led to a biologically conditioned morality, and finally from the religious vacuum of modern times. The cry for action, for dynamism, is no more than the positive expression of the demand that the artist be willing to sacrifice his life.

Kandinsky: dynamic abstraction

In 1912 the first great Futurist exhibition came to Munich. It added further fuel to the revolution in painting which Kandinsky had already begun in the circle of the *Blaue Reiter*. Kandinsky's early paintings are not especially promising. They are not so good as the early works of his Munich friends Marc and Macke, and they belong to a kind of Russian *Jugendstil* which is best represented by Leon Bakst. In politics as in art, the great innovators are not necessarily the most talented. Kandinsky is a case in point. What the innovator needs is the decisiveness that enables him to break radically with what has gone before; he needs a visionary imagination, self-confidence, and endurance. Kandinsky had all these qualities. In 1909 his paintings were still expressionistic notations of reality. From 1910 on, they are frequently called "Composition" or "Improvisation." They contain a certain musical element, which may have been intensified by Kandinsky's own love for music. Conversely, his contemporaries, such as Debussy and Scriabin liked to associate their musical compositions with colors. However, these artists were not working out a rational synthesis; rather, they were groping their way back to the emotional wellsprings of creation, where sound and color are both feeling and are, as yet, undistinguished from one another. "Pure sound exercises a direct impression on the soul. The soul attains to an objectless vibration." [21] But if we now glance at Kandinsky's pure abstractions of 1914 (**XXIII**), we shall find a much more specific image than we have been led to expect from his statement— a turbulent, explosive, violent image. These paintings, unlike those of French Cubism, show neither the basic figures of geometry nor a directly perceptible order. Here is what Kandinsky has to say about them: "Painting is a thundering collision of different worlds, destined to create a new world. Technically, every work comes into existence as the universe comes into existence, namely through catastrophes. Yet in the end the chaotic discord of the instruments makes for a symphony which we call music of the spheres." [22]

The cataclysmic character of the art of 1910

The last quotation shows that Kandinsky clearly recognized a tendency which we can observe in all countries around 1910: the birth of form is seen as a major upheaval. *The thundering collision of different worlds, the need for disharmony*—these are the sparks that kindle the creative flame. To be sure, these disquieting factors exist at all times, and frequently they are stronger than the sense of harmony perceived in the work of a Raphael or a Renoir. But around 1910 the artistic consciousness of catastrophe was closely related to scientific discoveries and to social and political events. It is not unusual for crises and conflicts to be sensed earlier and more sharply by the sensitive antennae of art than in the social and political spheres. Delaunay, the Futurists, Franz Marc, and Kandinsky expressed in their paintings their premonitions of catastrophe.

But these paintings of Kandinsky's are also dream-like and lyrical

because of the poetical and musical nature of their creator. They are both sublime and bombastic. Their explosiveness abolished, for the first time in Western art, the distance between the artist and his object, and in doing so they also eliminated the distance between artist and spectator. Instead, they include the spectator, thus achieving Marinetti's goal. Ground line and distance have disappeared, and the painting has become pure creation, pure action, to be re-experienced by the spectator.

The element of uncertainty

Form has turned into a "handwriting," and consists now of dots, blobs, hooks, twirls, crosses, and lines, all written in color. They are not derived from outer experience and cannot be checked by reason. An inner experience becomes visible: it is unique; it has never existed before and thus will never exist again. Such an art can only be savored by the spectator's aesthetic sensibility, whereas representational art used to evoke the whole breadth of human experience. We are therefore confronted with a radical reduction of the appeal of art and, at the same time, with a concentration on the wholly visual aspects of painting. We absorb the work of art purely through our aesthetically trained sense of vision, which may then pass on its experience to other areas of human insight. Whatever insights we may gain, they come to us neither through nature nor as literary content, as they have for thousands of years, but solely through associations evoked by sense impressions which cannot be rationally checked.

With Kandinsky, an element of uncertainty entered modern art. Are our interpretations right? Are our value judgments correct? These are the disturbing questions we ask as we face a work of art incommensurable with nature and disconnected from tradition. If we nevertheless enjoy, comprehend, and judge such works of art—despite our uncertainty—we do so on the basis of our general ability to experience aesthetic statements. Whatever Kandinsky may have expressed through his dots, lines, and colors, we participate in an awakening of sensuous-spiritual phenomena. What remains uncertain is merely how much of the artist's intention has reached us and whether we have understood correctly.

The element of ineffability

This cultural phenomenon of uncertainty is further intensified through that other cultural phenomenon—ineffability. Because Kandinsky and most of the painters after him do not refer to reality but instead produce a reality which has not existed before, our language actually lacks a vocabulary with which to describe such painting. Anyone who has not actually seen a nonobjective work of art will hardly be able to recognize it after having heard only a verbal description. The logical structure of syntax can at best only approximate an aesthetic statement. Descriptions of modern art are comparable to translations of Oriental poetry into Western languages; the structure of the European languages is so entirely different, that the result is a European poem with an Asian "mood." In the same way our critical language, circumscribed by logic as it is, is able only to isolate visual phenomena, compare them to related ones, and render the "mood" of the work; but no words can express modern art's actual, totally liberated structure. The meaning of modern art may be formulated, but its expression cannot be translated into the medium of words. We have spoken of the uncertainty of our understanding and of the ineffability of our impressions as cultural phenomena because we are not dealing with a private experience—an encounter between a work of art and its observer—but, rather, with a problem that involves the public role of art. Art criticism and all literary activity connected with art encounters this linguistic barrier with every abstract work of art.

We shall therefore not even attempt to give an exact account of what Kandinsky's paintings are; we shall restrict ourselves to describing their effects and the painter's means of achieving them. Kandinsky's early paintings look as if they had been hurled onto the canvas: the forms flow and spurt over the surface, hurried and oblique; an inner vision and an external shape have fused into one and owe little to nature. They communicate the experience of freedom, and this is why they fascinate us. They proclaim a state of anarchy with regard to the surrounding world, but show a sense of joyous responsibility toward the creative impulse. For this reason there is nothing accidental or disorderly about them, in spite of their stormy vehemence. Contrary to the popular misunderstanding, no child or amateur could ever paint anything like them.

Painting without a "handwriting"

During World War I, Kandinsky returned to Russia, where he came under the influence of the ideologies of the Suprematists and the Nonobjectivists. As a result, around 1920, he began to create Cubist-symbolic forms of a stern order. Although Kandinsky found in Munich the appropriate atmosphere for the development of his art and personality, his creative impulse essentially derived from a specifically Russian revolutionary radicalism, one which grew simultaneously with Cubism and Malevich's nonobjective painting in Moscow. In 1913 the Russian painter, Kasimir Malevich, exhibited a painting which consisted solely of a black circle against a white background. In 1918 he carried his position to its logical extreme, with the series "Suprematist Composition: White on White"—white-filled canvases. However, according to the artist, these were not simply blank surfaces, for they represented "the experience of nonobjectivity." It is easy to ridicule Malevich, but history has shown that the strong influence of Suprematism endures to this day. Therefore his paintings must have been based on creative, fertile ideas, as expressed in his credo: "There can be no question of 'painting' in Suprematism. Painting is a thing of the past, and the painter is a prejudice of the past. What we must do is turn directly to the masses of color as such and there look for the decisive forms. The movement of the red, green, and blue masses cannot be reproduced by means of representational drawing. This dynamism is simply a revolt of the aesthetic substance which has become independent and rebels against the object." [23]

What Malevich wished to express in words and paint is the rejection of the personal "handwriting" and sign language of the painter. Instead, he wanted to place before the eye the very activities of regular color areas, purged of everything personal. When he related these figures to experience, he called his paintings "Emotion of Flying," or "Feeling of Infinite Space"—that is, he associated them with those transpersonal experiences with which the twentieth century is familiar. It is strange that this hatred of the individual, together with the glorification of the machine, appeared first in Italy and in Russia. Social resentment, a rejection of the bourgeois-capitalistic world, and political anti-individualism undoubtedly fostered these currents. But no creative movement can draw its strength from negative sources alone. The historical dynamics of the new program, of the new vision, were anything but negative.

The aesthetics of engineering

This point becomes quite clear when we look at the paintings Malevich created after 1914, in which he arrived at a broader position. The geometric color planes are arranged diagonally, evoking the experience of motion and sequence in their spatial and temporal synthesis. At this point, the aesthetics of engineering enter the picture. The painter senses beauty in the sharpness, precision, and organization of engineering designs to which the pure unmixed colors lend an emotional vibration. From here we go only one step farther to arrive at a new spatial experience and thereby an enlarged aesthetic sensation which is achieved through transparence, diagonal projection, and fragmentary vanishing lines. This step was taken by Lissitzky, adapted by the stage directors Tairoff and Meyerhold, and further developed by Moholy-Nagy and others of the Bauhaus during the 1920's. They were all partially indebted to Suprematism, although their work stands in opposition to the antispatial and antitemporal mysticism embodied in the absolute color form of Malevich. We have reached a crossroads: one road led to the form experiments of engineering aesthetics; the other, to absolute painting with its purity of color. Engineering aesthetics does not proclaim freedom of individual expression; rather, as the exponent of a standardized society, it aims at a transpersonal correctness. As the Jesuit Naphtha says in Thomas Mann's *Magic Mountain*: "But if you believe that the result of future revolutions will be freedom, you are very much mistaken. The principle of freedom has reached its fulfillment and outlived itself by five hundred years."

Mondrian: the Platonism of absolute forms

Just as Malevich rejected the sign language of painting, so Mondrian rejects all personal expression that enters into the process of creating forms. "As long as the artistic process makes use of any 'form,' it will be impossible to create pure relations. For this reason, the new art will not mold any shapes." [24]
We might bear in mind that in France, in 1920, Picasso's friend, the poet Max Jacob, called for a dehumanization of art. Cryptically he wrote: "A personality is nothing but a persisting error." [25]

Mondrian had started out with objective paintings of Cubist sparseness but, as a consequence of these views, he turned in 1913 to bricklike stratifications with broken tones. In 1917-18, he and Theo van Doesburg carried these forms from atmospheric tone to pure color, and in 1921 he produced the first of those arrangements of color squares (**XXIV**) which for the next twenty years

were to express his search for the absolute. These subtly balanced horizontal and vertical lines are filled with the three primary colors—red, blue, and yellow—contrasting with white, grey, and black. Even when squares appear, the form, according to Mondrian, is neutralized "since they appear only as the result of horizontal and vertical lines which extend over the entire surface." [26] These rectangles and squares are not to be understood in terms of space for they are formed and separated by lines; nor can the colors come into "natural" contact with one another, for they, too, are separated and contrasted by the white and black lines. Here we have reached the purest form of a harmony of planes which is anti-Renaissance, asymmetrical, and nonobjective. Ultimately, Mondrian's and Van Doesburg's paintings are line-and-color patterns of great purity. This explains the mutual influence which the artists who, in 1917, formed in Holland the group *de Stijl* had on one another: they were four painters, a sculptor, and three architects. Van Doesburg created the floor patterns for a house built by J. J. P. Oud in Nordwigkerhout in 1917; the façades of Oud's and Rietveld's buildings, designed in the 1920's have a linear-square pattern of asymmetrical balance, while the furniture and floor plans are adaptations of Mondrian's art of planes. The ground plan of a country house by Mies van der Rohe (1922) looks like a painting by van Doesburg.[27]

The tentative Russian beginnings of the movement, realized only in trial models and in stagecraft, were soon destroyed by the social realism of Stalinist doctrine; but in the free West they led to a fusion of the arts not seen since the Baroque Age. What Mondrian and his circle (as well as the German Bauhaus group) envisioned was a "realized art"—that is to say, both painting and sculpture were to abandon their separate existence and come to life as part of their newly ordered surroundings. The barriers between the arts were to be broken down and there was to take shape a total reality in which everything would, in a sense, be art.

Thus, paradoxically, Platonic esotericism contributed to a heightened vitality in all areas of modern art. But it also gave rise to a question—one that will reverberate for a long time to come: Can art continue to serve as a heightened elucidation of human existence, or will it merely be an ornamental part of daily life?

The Bauhaus

Not only Dutch architecture and applied arts, but also the Bauhaus, founded by Gropius in 1919 in Weimar, became a world center of this new theory of form and its application. Van Doesburg, who taught in 1921 at the Bauhaus, acted as mediator of the "neoplastic" ideologies.

The contribution of the Bauhaus was twofold: first, it added a pedagogic dimension (for at the Bauhaus nonrepresentational art was *taught*); second, the Bauhaus masters created objects and buildings designed to express the age of technology by means of rationalization and standardization. The Nazi regime, when it closed the Bauhaus and forced its masters to emigrate, involuntarily helped its theories achieve a worldwide effect.

These theories concern themselves with the handling of structure, texture, and facture (the orderly arrangement of bodies of equal shape), transparence, perforation, penetration of spaces, and the mobility and density of objects in relation to light. The ground line as a point of departure for bodies in space is abandoned in favor of floating, stilt-supported, or freely hanging structures. Moholy-Nagy expounded this system of aesthetics in his book *Von Material zu Architektur* (Munich, 1928),[28] and Sigfried Giedion, applied it to contemporary civilization. Its purest demonstration can be seen in the norm-based architecture of Mies van der Rohe. Thus, the painting of Mondrian has led us back to architecture, along a route of symptomatic importance. For in its purism and radicalism Constructivist painting, developed between 1915 and 1920, pushed forward to its limits and, having reached them, encountered again an applied art: architecture. Painting, having become depersonalized and void of any "denotation," turned into formal designs which, because of their lack of content, could be used by allied arts. On the other hand, the basically geometric character of Constructivism had a natural affinity for architecture and machine products, since it had originally been inspired by the vocabulary of technology. The threads run in both directions, for the fabric is genuine.

De Stijl and the Bauhaus were purist movements. They rejected a definition like William Blake's *Exuberance is beauty* and replace it with one of biological appropriateness. At the same time they tended toward a technological grand gesture, which in the case of the Bauhaus led occasionally to the demonstration of fake technoforms which were not at all functional. It would seem that there is such a thing as a romanticism of the antiromantics.

But history has shown that even the extremes of Constructivist painting became productive in areas touching the other arts, precisely by virtue of their purism. These extremes, more than any other tendency of the new painting, have changed the face of our culture.

Formal variations of geometric abstractions are still being developed, and their principles have been absorbed by the applied arts and by architecture. Nevertheless, the initial fire has died down.

Klee: the magic hieroglyph

Although the art of free and geometric abstraction may still be considered in the light of basic principles, the work of Paul Klee defies any such categorization. While his work partakes of both free and geometric abstraction, it does not depend on either and it grows beyond both. It constitutes an exception, a diversion from the mainstream. Klee uses the fragile line as the direct agent of inner images, and in his mature work the design is the medium for expressing a trance-like inspiration. Klee partakes of a double experience: the play of his imagination, and the potential of line, color, and form, which reveal themselves, as it were, through him and beyond him. These lines and colors are the painted echo of a somnambulistic world experience, in which inside and outside, the *I* and the *Thou*, are as yet inseparable. Klee, his own inventor, could say rightly of himself: "On this side of the world I cannot be grasped at all. For I am at home with the dead as well as with the unborn; a little closer to the heart of creation than is customary." [29] The appropriate sign for such transcendence is the hieroglyph.

With no other artist of our time is this tendency to invent a world so much directed toward an interchange of form and intuition. Tracing the paths of point and line, of triangle and spiral, of pink and silver, Klee gropes his way into a realm of ethereal creatures. The "Garden of Orpheus" opens before him. The grotesque and the paradoxical make their appearance as hitherto unexplored possibilities of creation. Yet the conception does not actually come from the creator but from his empathy with the genesis of the first image or initial form. Consider a canvas covered from top to bottom with colored stripes of varying size. A few narrow toward the top and therefore give the impression of vanishing lines. Here and there delimiting lines rise vertically above a horizontal one—and convey the impression of steps. With only semiconscious will, the artist now explores these suggestions. Gently he pursues the motive, until it at last reveals itself as "Highway and Byways" (1929; **XXV**).

This painting demonstrates that a mosaic-like surface can simultaneously be a "highway and byways." Klee shows us that reality is but the result of a point of view, of a perspective. He has given us a magic sign for the feeling implied by the title. What we have known as an experience, has now become an image. Klee makes

feeling visible in the sign; he is indeed the purest painter of a priori feeling, which is neither reality nor abstraction but something in between. Klee's pictures belong neither to reality nor to abstraction, but to an inbetween world which is the birthplace of the creative act. In most finished works this road station marking the artist's pursuit of his image has been eliminated; in Klee's work it remains as the content itself. This is what constitutes his gentle and yet daemonic uniqueness.

Surrealism

Klee shares with Surrealism the belief in the magical power of transformation inherent in the symbol. But while Klee puts the translogical element in the service of emotion and aims at a final, pure certainty, Surrealism uses art as an instrument of the paradox, the enigma, the absurd. However, we must add immediately —and paradoxically—that the absurd makes sense, that it is anything but nonsense. The "surreality" of Surrealism stems from modern man's sense of doubt and suffering when confronted with reality. This doubt has its roots in an awareness that the objective world depends for its existence on a subject—that is, on a thinking, perceiving individual. Kant provided a philosophical clarification of this subjectivity of the experience of the objective and, with it, brought much suffering to the Romantics. Schopenhauer divided the world into Will and Idea. Finally, Freud demonstrated—although with a fanatical insistence on the sexual basis of the "will"—that the mind's ability to create order rests on unconscious, instinctive drives which reveal themselves only through symbols.

The absurd and the transrational are powerful in the same way that dreams are powerful, but only art can shape such intangible realities as desire and renunciation. This is the domain which Surrealism has staked out for itself. Here the suprareality of the dream and the subreality of nonsense merge and by it a fusion of intuition and nihilism takes place.

De Chirico: *pittura metafisica*

Around 1911 the Italian painter Giorgio de Chirico initiated *pittura metafisica*. He elucidated the basic experiences of his metaphysics in the language of Cubism, which had just come into being: "The silence of infinite spaces," the paralysis of time, the interchangeability of illusion and reality, "the inanimate and quiet beauty of matter." "The Great Metaphysician" (1917; Museum of Modern Art, New York) shows a tower of heterogeneous cubes, chests, frames, and saw-marked wooden forms. The Cubism of Picasso and Braque has been transformed into a sculptured monument to the desolation and anxiety of existence. Every human being is familiar with this sense of desolation; courage, inventiveness, and a creative will are required to express it. But because these are the very qualities that will overcome desolation, a paradox is created: nihilism is refuted in the very process of being proclaimed.

The mannequin, here the symbol of a godless and senseless existence, rules a world composed of extremely severe forms. The clarity and consistency of the vision give it power. We are dealing now with the close relationship between nihilism and aestheticism—a relationship explicitly affirmed by de Chirico himself, who rested his case on Schopenhauer and Nietzsche. In the deadly paralysis of the noon hour, his objects live a specter-like life of their own. Deprived of their function, they are nothing but sculptural bodies, which can enter into new and unexpected—that is, surrealistic—relations with other forms.

Dada

Dada goes a step farther: it uses paradox as a weapon. Its goal is to kill the meaning of the object and usher in the aesthetic freedom to create functionless shapes, and to show the absurdity of existence, including art, by means of absurd images. It is well known how Dadaism came into being in 1916 in Zürich, in the revolutionary atmosphere surrounding a group of young anti-militarists, anarchists, and nihilists. André Breton, the literary standard-bearer of Surrealism, points out that Dada, as a mani-festation of antiwar defeatism, had antecedents in similar times of crisis—for instance, during the aftermath of the Franco-Prus-sian War of 1870-71, with Lautréamont and Rimbaud.

Stylistically Dada derives from Italian Futurism and from French Cubism. Its scope extends from the inspired cynicism of Marcel Duchamp and Max Ernst to the genuinely daemonic transforma-tions that take place in the world created by Franz Kafka. At about this time Kafka wrote *The Worries of a Family Man*, which deals with a creature named Odradek, who looks like a spool of thread and lives a marginal existence on a staircase. Kafka's pre-cise and profound vision of the abyss has given us a metaphysics of Surrealism for which Dada created a cynical counterimage.

The conscious vs. the unconscious

But Surrealism is also indebted to the visionary dream power of such masters as Redon, Ensor, and Henri Rousseau. Rousseau had a particularly far-reaching effect. True magic can begin only where form itself helps to effect the metamorphosis, and such is the case with Rousseau, in whose paintings there appears for the first time the unintended freezing of time and the petri-faction of space. This is the result of an ideographic depiction of the visible world like those produced by children and primitive cultures. In the naïve yet infinitely subtle art of the "Douanier" Rousseau both the child and the early stages of artistic expression remain preserved; it was these elements that held such attraction for the contemporary artist. The Surrealists, however, were to use this type of vision to symbolize paradox and the disintegration of the world.

Contemporary critics who take a religious or conservative viewpoint use *paradox* and *disintegration* as condemnation of this art. But, the artist experiences this disintegration as a reality of life and by giving form to his experience he proves to those who cannot or will not admit its existence that it is a power in the midst of us. If his creation is articulate, it has already gained a positive aesthetic value, for it takes issue and gives form to what has been formless. André Breton rightly demands that Surrealism be understood as a search for a meeting ground of *coincidentia oppositorum*, and that for this reason the concepts of "constructive" and "destructive" should no longer be used as weapons against one another.[30]

Surrealism developed during the 1920s and must, to an extent, be viewed in the context of the intellectual climate of that decade: a world war was over; the Russian Revolution had destroyed the spiritual and economic foundations of Eastern Europe; millions of people were displaced; the West, rebelling against restraint, reacted by releasing its repressed urge for freedom. Whatever was not expressly forbidden was allowed. Neither victors nor vanquished could discern meaning or purpose.

The theory of Surrealism rests on the newly discovered realm of the unconscious. Much has been said about the passive states of sleep and intoxication, in which the artist supposedly becomes a willing medium of the unconscious. But the paintings of the Surrealists display none of the many-layered entanglement of the unconscious mind that Joyce tried to reproduce in literary form. On the contrary, they show a heightened clarity of the dream image that can only be the result of a wide-awake self-consciousness. Sigmund Freud shrewdly commented to Salvador Dali: "What interests me about your art is not the unconscious but the conscious." [31]

The art of Klee and Kandinsky is much more an art of the un-conscious than surrealism ever was. What the Surrealists write about themselves must not be confused with what they actually paint. Marx Ernst, one of the few Surrealists who have proven themselves capable of stylistic growth, brings us close to the sources of the Surrealist imagination: "When one brings two dis-tant realities together on an apparently antipathetic plane, an exchange of energy transpires, provoked by the very meeting." [32]

Dali: illusionism

This happens most consistently in the paintings of Salvador Dali, in which are found not only enigmatic beings and shapes, but also ambiguous picture-puzzles which take on various meanings and appearances, depending on the point of view of the spectator. Seen in a different re-composition of forms, the contour of a mountain turns out to be a human face. The image changes its meaning and, as a result, our own point of view begins to vacil-late. As André Breton writes: "A tomato is also a child's balloon —Surrealism, I repeat, having suppressed the word *like*." [33]

In addition, Dali's paintings open into infinite depths of space, so that the objects are seen as through the wrong end of a tele-scope: diminutively, but with the greatest precision. In dreams, too, objects sometimes acquire an abnormal sharpness which surpasses all experiences of our conscious sight in its incredible exactitude. This abnormal sharpness of vision, coupled with a completely enigmatic content, is what Dali calls "handmade color photography of concrete irrationality." The spectator is to be per-suaded to recognize an unknown reality in the painting and a secret meaning in what is sheer fantasy. Such meaning indeed exists, insofar as shape and space may in themselves express childhood fears, erotic fantasies, psychological complexes, or cultural reminiscences for which rational imagery offers no anal-ogies. In fact, Dali's work, made up of bluff and inspiration and realized with a high degree of technical skill, is quite inimitable

(XXVI). In the final analysis, the absence of true conviction in his work leaves only the qualities of emptiness and sensationalism. In the 1920's and 1930's, however, Dali's influence on artists of all countries was great, for he literally revealed new horizons of art.

Aside from its content, Dali's surrealism must be credited with having kept alive the classical art of drawing and the presentation of perspectivic space under the flood of often amorphous abstractions. It is a historic fact that every art of illusionism has used an extreme realism, sharpening it to a fine point in order to achieve the illusion of illusion. Dali's paintings, unlike contemporary art in general, are windows that open onto a different space. In this respect Dali and his followers belong completely to the past or, as Gertrude Stein said pungently in her book about Picasso: "The Surrealists still see things as every one sees them, they complicate them in a different way but the vision is that of every one else, in short the complication is the complication of the twentieth century but the vision is that of the nineteenth century. . . . Complications are always easy but another vision than that of all the world is very rare." [34]

But at the basis of Surrealism there is a point of view and a method so definite that it can also be expressed—and perhaps more fruitfully—in nonrepresentational painting. In this context we shall have to return to Surrealism once more.

Chagall: painter of myths

The painters of myths of our century, Chagall and Beckmann, are related to representational Surrealism through the element of fantasy, although the content of their art is entirely different from that of Surrealism. They are tellers of myths, whereas Surrealism only conjures up trick images of dreams to comment on the disintegration of the world in terms of ambiguity and paradox.

Chagall's work, like that of Kandinsky, is determined by the painter's childhood impressions and his mystic-religious Russian background (Greek Orthodox in Kandinsky's case, Jewish Orthodox in Chagall's case). Readers familiar with Martin Buber's collections of Hassidic stories will recognize in Chagall's work the same mixture of faith, miracle, and down-to-earth wit. Yet it was neither Russia nor Poland, but Paris, that protected and developed this heritage. Only in Paris could Chagall put the primitive and child-like elements of his style into a valid contemporary context. He still speaks, both in form and in content, of the impressions of his youth; white-haired, he remains a child prodigy. He tells of his village and its inhabitants, of lovers and bridal couples, and in later years he also tells of the fall of Lucifer and of the Crucifixion. His human beings have as few bones, muscles, and joints as the votive figures scattered over the European countryside; rightly his people can float and dive without violating the laws of gravity. They are creatures of inspiration and witnesses to miracles. Human being, animal, candle, clock (**XXVII**), violin, and Torah take part in creation and enter into miraculous combinations and relations. Chagall's color scheme is originally indebted to that of Delaunay and French *Orphisme*, but he has enriched it with violets, yellows, and reds known only in the ritual of the Russian Church. Thus he adds a liturgical element to the dynamism of pure color. To a higher degree than in Cubism, "optical transparence" becomes "spiritual transparence," to use the words of one of his biographers, Georg Schmidt. We do not need to know whether Chagall professes a belief in God. We do, however, feel his instinctive and intuitive faith, for his paintings bear witness to it. The difference between Chagall and such a painter as Rouault lies in the fact that the latter paints modern icons, reviving and reformulating Byzantine Christian art; his meaning is predetermined and he repeats and enriches it with a dogged obstinacy. With Chagall, on the other hand, everything is inspiration. Nothing is known ahead of time, everything is the gift of the inspired hour. His art does not ask the spectator to believe, but only to sympathize—to join in the joy and pain of others.

Beckmann: the new Prometheus

From a formal viewpoint it does not make much sense to mention Max Beckmann in the same breath as Chagall. It would seem more appropriate to connect Chagall with Chaim Soutine, who comes from a similar milieu. But the Northern, German Expressionist Beckmann shares with Chagall the experience of the miraculous and the mythical. Other than that, their artistic backgrounds and their visual language are fundamentally different. Beckmann's personality and art are essentially determined by his will—by the thrust of a colossal ambition.

He began his career with the depiction of nude figures in the open air and with incisive portraits: psychological sensitivity on one side, the fully developed artistic means of late Impressionism on the other. But the war experience destroyed this orderly and inherited world for the soldier-painter, and he began to parallel the Expressionists, who were of his generation. The paintings of Henri Rousseau introduced him to the world of magic which he was never again to leave. But his metamorphosis of reality arises from an unusual and passionate love-hate empathy. His is not the work of a dreamer, but of a seer. Not by accident did Dostoevsky, with his probing interest in horror, exert a formative literary influence on Beckmann at this time. Although the artist's mundane metropolitan paintings have a satirical tone, they do not accuse. His colors are not taken from nature and his forms, with their unwieldy design and squeezed composition, are anticlassical. They recall the jazz music of the 1920's. But they go beyond jazz in their daemonic ability to evoke pity and terror. These paintings seem to shout, scream, and shriek, and at the same time they are chained, mutilated, and petrified. Since Brueghel there has been no more painful a fool's world than that of Beckmann. The famous "Self-Portrait in Tuxedo" (1927; Busch-Reisinger Museum, Cambridge, Massachusetts) reveals how the artist wanted to be regarded at that time: as the anti-bohemian, the scrutinizer disguised as the man-about-town.

At the beginning of the 1930s, a change took place and Beckmann became less concerned with specific and transient phenomena and more preoccupied with the typical. His types derive their sensuous conviction from the painter's intrusive empathy with the object, whether landscape or portrait, and they acquire substance from his brooding expansion of the world's myths. The great triptychs of Beckmann's later years are the final result. The tripartite form itself is in the tradition of religious painting, but the Christian triptych stated a familiar content while Beckmann developed a private mythology. What Heraclitus said about the oracle of Delphi holds true for these bold paintings: "The god whose oracle is at Delphi uses neither words nor silence, but insinuations." The first of these paintings is called "Departure" (1932-35; Museum of Modern Art, New York; **XXVIII**). Beckmann painted it before he voluntarily left Hitler's Germany in 1937. The center panel depicts a blue ocean with a boat in which sit the crowned Fisher King, a woman and child, and a companion whose head is shrouded in a hood. The two side panels carry associations with the forms and themes of the 1920's: men and women who are tied, gagged, mutilated; a blindfolded bell boy. The classical world of repose (though a phantom shares the boat) is set up against an image of violated mankind. In the triptych, "Blindmans Buff" (1945; Minneapolis Art Institute), this theme is taken up once more. A group of musicians occupies the center, while the side panels show the blind, the blinded, the blindfolded. The center panel symbolizes life affirming itself; the sides, the existence of those who live without sight.

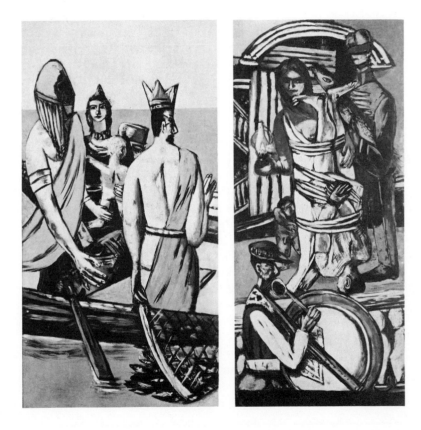

PAINTING

In most of Beckmann's paintings the affirmation is concentrated in the center—sometimes as a chained painter (St. Anthony), an actor, or an acrobat—while the sides recurringly symbolize the repression of the instincts straining for freedom and the senseless attraction of the sensual world. The color attains a certain nobility, but the form remains unwieldy, as if it were groaning. The bodies are always crowded, depriving one another of space, almost as though they were in prison. Perhaps this crush and press of bodies serves as protection against the threat of space—the absolute void. The painter shields himself against infinity behind physical, sensual shapes. This is the ultimate gesture of Beckmann's love of reality and his cosmic fear, his *Weltangst*. Willingly or not, he is a modern Prometheus, chained to his truth.

Picasso: the modern Proteus

If Beckmann is the Prometheus of our time, Picasso is its Proteus. He is neoclassicist, cubist, surrealist, but each in his own way; he has more than paid back any debt he owes to other masters and other cultures. When he is cheerful, he loves to play with masks and disguises, a game that poses the question: Am I this? Am I that? And his every work contains both this question and a provisional answer. This is what Picasso meant when he said: "Art is a lie that makes us realize truth." [35] In contrast to the abstract Expressionists of a younger generation, Picasso takes for his starting point an impression of art or reality, from which his work evolves in a gradually advancing and drawn-out genesis. He allows us to glimpse this process of evolution in long series of paintings, prints, and drawings. These series reveal how he fragmentizes the original model, isolates the parts and uses them as building stones for a new reality, and finally reorganizes them in an order that is neither emotional nor organic but primarily formal. For "through art we express our conception of what is nature not." [36]

A work of so experimental a nature, which does not aim at reproducing visible reality but only uses it as material for a new reality, rids itself of the organic, indissoluble, objective, and psychological cohesion of the visible world—of that world which has fired the painter's imagination from Giotto to Matisse. Therefore Picasso can say: "I try to make any object abandon its usual function. I take a thing up only at the point when it is worth no more than a piece of junk that has ceased to be useful." Hence his well-known figures made of old pipes and boards, his monkeys put together with children's toys. This is not the surrealism which, through derangement, opens up new perspectives on reality but, rather, the Protean expression of metamorphosis. Reality challenges the artist, as if it wanted to have its components playfully shuffled and rearranged by him: "Picasso, creater of tragic toys for adults!"[37]

The meaning of deformation

What is so surprising about this metamorphosis is Picasso's style, which ranges from a Mediterranean gracefulness to terrifying deformation. This deformation not only ignores organic nature, but it even attacks the "aesthetic," the "beautiful" as such. As Werner Haftmann puts it: "The repulsive, with its shock action, breaks through the barrier which beauty sets up round the human drama." [38] Picasso draws the final conclusion from Baudelaire's observation: "Whatever is not distorted in a certain manner is an object of indifference; therefore that which is irregular—that is, the unforeseen, the abrupt, the surprising—are essential and characteristic elements of beauty."[39]

Deformation can then be either a "characteristic element of beauty" or the opposite: an expression of the fact that form no longer attempts to be aesthetically pleasing but, rather, seeks to arouse through shock. Picasso's art ranges from a playful aestheticism to a painful fetishism. It transcends the boundaries of any given style and conveys entirely new experiences. His noble classical figures (derived from the paintings at Pompeii), which swell to hideous dimensions or assume an elongated, spindle-like appearance, are the heralds of horror and panic. Distortion and color turn the simple objects of a still-life into symbols of terror, fear, ecstasy, or hysteria.

Brought together, these objects and figures become a form of picture-writing, as in the great fresco-like "Guernica" (1937; owned by the artist, on loan to the Museum of Modern Art, New York), in which Picasso demonstrates that the contemporary artist can very well raise an outcry against hate and horror and become the spokesman of the struggle against tyranny. The politically conditioned realism which characterizes the art of Communist and Fascist societies and periods has produced nothing to compare with the pathos and power of Picasso's picture-writing. Although it may seem a paradox, freedom and human dignity are today preserved only in an art which denies its dependence on nature.

However extreme his distortions or great the variety of his technical solutions, Picasso himself can always find his way back to the model in nature or art, for he preserves the stages of the metamorphosis in the final image. Yet, in spite of this, Picasso had had a tremendous influence on the destruction of the natural model. He had proven that the deformation of nature can, in its own way, be formally just as constructive as the use of organic natural forms and in doing so, he has added to the building materials of art with an infinite store of possibilities: he has proclaimed a freedom beyond nature. Art will return to nature only when it again finds it more rewarding to interpret optic reality than to create a language of forms which relates directly to the inner nature of man.

Picture-writing: its reappearance

Picture-writing and magical symbols have no place in an art tied to nature; they belong only to the earliest stages of a civilization. But they break through the surface once more when the possibilities of naturalism—including a naturalistic classicism like that of Greek art—have been exhausted. Thus they appeared toward the end of ancient history and again in the twentieth century. The magical symbol no longer has an objective cultural or religious content; instead, it emerges spontaneously from the ego and 'id' of the artist thimself. The language of this picture-writing is not taught in schools; its symbols refer to no given, established content, and their appeal is not to the conscious mind. But how are we to interpret a hieroglyphic writing that is not based on common convention? If we look for such a convention in a definable content, we shall certainly not find it. If, however, we try to understand such hieroglyphs in terms of the instinctive agreement that exists between the human psyche and the creative play of nature, we may enter the world of images to which the painting provides a key. Encouraged by Paul Klee, who entrusted himself to spontaneous symbolism, the painters of today have sent out thousands of pictorial signals and have made art more and more the record of an inner imagery. Among these, two stand out: Kandinsky (in his late phase), and the Spaniard, Juan Miró.

Kandinsky and Miró: the microcosmic imagination

As a teacher in Dessau, doubtless influenced by constructivism and the Bauhaus ideology, Kandinsky turned from free expression to geometric expression. It is fascinating to observe how a pictorial space gradually comes to surround these playful forms on an abstract plane until square, circle, and line no longer stand *upon* a surface, in the manner of known and orderly objects, but float and move *in* the picture. A biological metamorphosis seems to have set in. In Kandinsky's paintings of the 1930's and 1940's, these organisms range from microbes with wings and tail to formal shapes that are reminiscent of those in Indian sand paintings. Kandinsky has left behind his Constructivist origins and is arranging the shapes of his imagination according to musical and rhythmic principles.

Miró, too, creates such signs and signals. He started out under the influence of Dali and French Surrealism, but he atomized the spatial unity in Dali. The individual signals streak across the canvas like comets, or bounce and roll over the surface. A Puck-like spirit haunts and conjures them. But Miró's style, too, changed at the beginning of the 1930's. The humorous element has given way to runic drawings, not unlike those in the late work of Klee (**XXIX**). Miró, like Klee, uses the color red and black as symbols of blood, fire, and death. In addition, Miró now invents shapes that derive from Arp's sculptures. Indeed, these shapes have become veritable trademarks of a kind of abstract *art nouveau*, a biomorphic art of ornamentation which has left its traces even on bar tables and "mobile" lamps. The organic sign and the ornamental game are closely linked in Miró's work. The ornament assimilates the power of formation and transformation inherent in the biological organism, and the freely invented hieroglyphs organize into floating groups.

An art of this type was envisioned by Juan Gris in 1923, but rejected by him for a reason which deserves to be considered today: "If I particularize pictorial relations to the point of representing objects, it is in order that the spectator shall not do so for himself, and in order to prevent the combination of colored forms from suggesting to him a reality which I had not intended." [40]

Art: the expression of the unintended

Such an unintended reality is now no longer avoided but, rather, sought. Is unintended reality identical with chance? Certainly, from the point of view of the artist and spectator. But where does the unintentional element come from? It appears with the first inroads the artist makes into intact matter, with the creative act,

with the relation between action and resulting form. This movement is both muscular and psychic and the resultant form is a script of colored tracings. But once it comes into being, the script is no longer subject to the will of its creator; rather, it becomes an independent shape sending back its own signals which, in turn, again evoke the creative impulse. Thus the painting as a whole can be seen as the result of psychoenergetic calls and responses. Such a description may well be disconcerting, for it renounces the hitherto recognizable characteristics of human civilization: the will and a consciously imposed meaning.

Yet the procedure described is not truly novel, for the part played by the unconscious and the accidental elements has always been much greater than some historians believe. In every creative act unforeseen discoveries are brought to the surface through sounds, words, colors, and lines. No genuine work of art is ever the mere description of a thought or the mere depiction of an idea or an impression. Formal signs serve not only as a means of communication with the spectator, but also as roads leading to new vistas for the artist, inviting him to undertake those journeys on which the essential adventure of art is experienced. Histories of art and literature cannot tell us much about these journeys, because they proceed from the finished product and its structures. But the artist has experienced his work as a developing process, and he knows something of the accidents and chance happenings that occurred along the way.

Nonrepresentational art: its comprehensibility

Now a question arises. Can the seismographic sign language we have discussed be deciphered, or is the spectator forced to leave empty-handed because of the artist's arbitrariness and subjectivity? Possibly, we feel the same uneasiness experienced by Juan

Gris in the early stages of abstract art. But, unexpectedly perhaps, we can find at least partial reassurance. A formal statement, by virtue of its existence, has the power to affect and to change us. Abstract painting, with and in spite of its soliloquies, has succeeded in creating a worldwide optical language. The shapes of a Kandinsky, a Miró, a Pollock, or a Kline gradually and imperceptibly enter our aesthetic awareness, much as a tree "settles" in us and assumes an inner meaning. But because Pollock's shapes did not exist before Pollock, we can understand and judge them only by what they themselves, and not anything or anybody else, have to say. As an American critic has put it: "A new imagery creates among other things the very standards by which alone it can be judged."[41]

Total aestheticism

However, the fact that every formal statement has the power to affect and to change us has an inherent limitation. For example, a rubbing of tree bark and a photograph of genes also contain statements about form: the one demonstrates texture; the other, a geometric or rhythmic order. Photographers have discovered and revealed the formal expressive value of torn posters, lattice fences, oil puddles, and pistons. In short, we have entered into an age of complete aestheticism. But if everything visible can be experienced as form and expression—and abstract art has taught us that this is indeed the case—then other questions arise: Where does the achievement of art begin? What is the contribution of the artist? Indeed, there exists an anarchist group among artists which would willingly reject existing definitions of art (as the Dada movement did). These are artists who no longer wish to create meaningful objective correlatives, but who see the finished work merely as a fragment of a film of consciousness continuously projected within them. For such artists, art is basically no more than a series of Rorschach tests through which they hope to interpret themselves.

Form: byproduct of expression

Our exhibitions are filled with such works. They are aesthetically interesting and deserve evaluation. But when all is said and done, their aim is not form at all, but liberated expression. Thus we are confronted by shapes which also happen to be form, but not because an act of the will imposed the form nor because they are related to a model or to a vision. Like the tree bark rubbing and the microscopic photograph of the genes, their aesthetic shape is only an incidental byproduct.

How did this genre come to be? The visible world has ceased to be a source of inspiration for the painter, exactly as it did toward the end of classical antiquity. We can check this against our own experience: If at an art gallery we walk from a room filled with contemporary paintings into one filled with nineteenth-century naturalistic paintings we may find that what once seemed fresh and expressive now strikes us as stale and insignificant. Thus abstraction has turned into a positive value; pure imitation of reality is no longer possible. The liberation of color and line from the tyranny of the visible object reflects the vitality and boundless individualism of our time.

Painting: the musical phase

Painting has definitely entered its "musical phase." Seurat and Gauguin perceived analogies between music and painting; Kandinsky and Klee sought a meeting ground between the two. Their vision has become reality: painting now is expression through color and shape, as music is expression through sound. We have long taken it for granted that musical sounds have a life of their own, that they create their own content, that they do not have to imitate natural sounds, such as the murmuring of a brook.

But we have learned only recently that colors, lines, and form can also express themselves, and that they constitute—in themselves—artistic content. Of course, the *how* and the *what* of the language of color is quite different from the language of sound. Under no circumstance can a blue "stand" for a given sound (the error of the symbolists). The relationship between music and painting must be seen not as a direct correlation; rather, it must be discovered and explored through their independent but parallel language of forms. Beyond this, painting and music also meet in their common rejection of hitherto valid systems of order. Surely it is no accident that the first nonrepresentational paintings were created by Kandinsky at the same time (1911-12) that Arnold Schönberg produced his first atonal compositions.

This positive discovery of the independent life of forms springs from the conviction that the representation of reality through art is no longer possible, because such representation presupposes that reality is static and determinable, and we have no certainty that such a reality even exists. Potential reality is revealed only within the creative process, during which it discovers itself.

Art as illusion is rejected on both ethical and aesthetic grounds, and representation as a bridge between nature and art is eliminated. Today the impressions received from nature and the expressions provided by art face one another disconnectedly. Nature and history must first enter into the artist's inner life before they can again become externalized. If an artist has the world within himself, his creations will reflect that world; if he does not, his painting will be no more than a series of monomaniac gestures. The nineteenth century glutted itself with undigested reality, but the twentieth century faces a dearth of reality, an insufficiency of content, concept, matter, and idea.

Maximal and minimal expression

However, it is not only the structure, but also the texture and,

PAINTING

chiefly, the "facture"—to use the Bauhaus terminology—which determine the expressive power of nonrepresentational painting. There has arisen a veritable aesthetic pathology of texture—painted surfaces that have been scratched, cut, burnt, seared—evocative of aggression and pain. This is the extreme of maximal values—mutilation of the surface of the painting as a means of expression. At the other extreme, minimal form and color changes take place against a monotonous background and monochromatic color plane. The neutrality of the background enhances the seismographic expressiveness of the form. For example, an announcement of a New York gallery shows the painter Adolph Gottlieb using a window-washer's squeegee to lay paint in uniform, textureless coatings (**XXX**). Laid thus against a neutral surface, the painted image stands forth as form. Gottlieb and artists like him deprive a painting of much of its "handwriting" in order to point up the suprapersonal reality of the form, the aesthetic sign (not unlike what Mondrian and Malevich had in mind). By contrast, the "action painters" attack the canvas, dripping, rubbing, wiping, throwing, thrusting, hitting, in order to engage painter, paint, and painted surface in a mental-physical interplay. At the pole opposite from Gottlieb's textureless application of color we find Jackson Pollock, who dribbled paint on canvas from above (**XXXI**). If the one completely deprived painting of gesture, the other turned painting into pure gesture. The art of abstract expressionism lies between these extremes. It is possible to group the various artistic productions and to make distinctions between them, but we have been concerned here not so much with assigning to each artist a definite place on a scale as with showing possible modes of creative expression.

Abstract Expressionism: variants

Probably one of the most important reasons why nonrepresentational art is so widespread and so persistent within a culture that was in no way prepared for it is that there is no limit to the independent form and color signs that can be invented. Discovery of the self, discovery of the world, freedom from rules, conventions, traditions—what a field of action for the artist! We shall begin our considerations with an area that lies still within the reach of verbal circumscription, an area that allows us to trace a connection back to the familiar symbols of geometric order and organic nature. The painters of constellations of geometric forms are clearly indebted to the rational aesthetics of the Bauhaus on the one hand and to Cubism on the other. The German-American Albers, the Swiss Bill, the German Schlemmer, the Hungarian Vasarely, and the Swiss Fritz Glarner all work within the Bauhaus tradition, while the British Pasmore and particularly Ben Nicolson continue the tradition of Cubism from which they derive ultimate refinements of spatial, coloristic, and linear values. The *I* bows out before the *id*, and an orderly, decorative element comes to predominate; the aim is still "beauty," aesthetic pleasure.

Those painters whose inspiration comes from living organisms also stand within a tradition and have ties that put them within reach of our words. These are the painters who derive their form from the encounter with the human being. Willem de Kooning definitely proceeds from the same ground as the Flemish Expressionists such as Constant Permeke. That is, his art is earthy, sensual, and provocative. Yet the human figure is only temporarily revealed and can be withdrawn at any moment back into the eddying stream of color. Karel Appel, likewise a Dutchman, shows with a heavier application of color the same zestful aggressiveness in his vibrant canvases (**XXXII**). In both of them one feels a certain love-hate toward the human form.

The Mexican painter Rufino Tamayo permits us a glance at the organic world, as does the German Fritz Winter. Between the experience of reality and the abstractions that have grown from it, a luminous space opens up, where mind and nature merge.

The work of the Russian-French painter Nicolas de Stael gives us perhaps the most impressive insight into this transformation as it takes place on the canvas itself. The actual theme of this outstanding colorist is the ambivalence of the mental and formal perception of nature, the transition from nature to color-sign. A group of California painters, among whom Richard Diebenkorn stands out (**XXXIII**), has gone in the opposite direction and has shown how abstractions can serve as a point of departure from which to go back into nature. Abstract constellations of form and color are reapplied to reality, and the canvas "postulates" the world. Whereas the Cubists of 1910 abstracted from a real still-life, now a painting begun as an abstraction or constructed in accord with abstract principles, is gradually led back to reality. Instead of the visual image's leading to abstraction, the abstraction projects itself into nature. This method of creating is likely to play a highly important role in the future. Picasso says of it: "There are painters who make of the sun a yellow splotch, but there are also those painters who, thoughtfully and with skill, make out of a yellow splotch a sun." [42]

Related but more abstract are those paintings which demonstrate with utmost subtlety the creative state of response and inspiration by means of floating substances that emerge from the painting ground. The Italian Afro (Balsadella) creates such poetic or musical images of fluctuating color. Fluctuation may become condensed into a rune, a calligraphic symbol, even a magic symbol. Willi Baumeister created such petroglyphs of the unconscious; in American art they can be seen in the early work of Adolph Gottlieb and in the colored visions of William Baziotes.

Christian faith inspires Alfred Manessier, who achieves a rare harmony of spontaneity and discipline. His paintings have some of the solemnity of medieval stained glass windows. Art of the Far East makes much use of the calligraphic symbol as a basic meeting ground of *I* and *world*, of a subjective expression which

XXXII. Appel, "Thunderbirds" (1960)

nevertheless attempts to make a statement that reaches beyond the *I*. In fact, quite a number of Japanese painters and calligraphers can be proven to have acted as mediators. On America's West Coast, with its vista on the Far East, the tendency toward an East-West synthesis is far advanced in the work of Morris Graves and his older master Mark Tobey. In Tobey's so-called white writing, the ego reveals itself in a spiderweb of light, which can be read as the tracings of mental and physical impressions (**XXXIV**). In his earlier work the sources of reality in the graphic net are identifiable; one can see the optical origins of this web of light that unfolds and devours itself. In his later work, only the light-calligraphy is left.

Related to him, but coloristically more fertile if more grotesque, is Jean Dubuffet, whose work carries an element of Klee's primitive magic. He may be called the "sorcerer of the scribbles on the wall" (Leonardo himself recommended the contemplation of graffitti as a stimulant to the imagination). Infantilism and sophistication combine in his paintings. A dot-and-splotch writing reports the unconscious in the work of the German Julius Bissier and in that of the Frenchman Henri Michaux. Reminiscent of the works of Paul Klee, their conscious content is more diminished if not absent altogether. A dreaming hand seems to have created these poetic improvisations.

The colored sign language of André Masson belongs between calligraphy and facture. Masson is among the most gifted artists of this type, as is the Russian-American Arshile Gorky. Gorky's art, initially closely related to Picasso and surrealism, went through many changes and had a strong influence on younger artists. He is a master of the free manipulation of a welter of forms, characterized by an almost anthropomorphic vitality. His forms fly, blossom, luxuriate; they seem even to chuckle and scream. In an inexplicable manner he manages to suggest an analogy with human experiences, his work therefore being spoken

of as "form surrealism." Unlike the modern inventors of the hieroglyph—Klee, Kandinsky, Miró—the abstract expressionists do not isolate the symbol, but make it part of an over-all pattern which originates in reactions to the outer and inner world.

Finally there are the *Tachists* and the "action painters": for them the canvas is no longer the primary artistic working condition upon which and by means of which a painting can evolve. Instead, the canvas becomes an arena for the painter and his actions. They use ever larger canvases in order to obtain a greater area for active expression. The fact that there exist few walls equal to such enormous canvases shows how sociologically uprooted this type of painting is.

Jackson Pollock may be regarded as one of the first and most gifted exponents of this group—in his radical break with tradition, Pollock introduced aluminum emulsions as a new painting medium, for he wanted to avoid the historical associations connected with oil painting. By sometimes dripping his paints from above onto the horizontal canvas, Pollock heightened the entanglement and density of the color web; the result is a kind of aesthetic chaos that contemplates itself. He does not recognize form as order, nor idea as definable concept—and yet the final product is unified, in its own way, and expressive in a novel manner. A meaningful gesture has come out of untamed revolt. Ultimately, there cannot be any genuine artistic gesture which does not bear witness to its creator's store of riches. We ourselves, endowed with an organizing vision, tend to infuse meaning into a painting, instinctively seeing form and expression wherever there is movement upon a surface. Thus it is hard to say where Pollock's work ends and ours begins. The same is true of the nervous gesticulations of Wols (Wolfgang Schulze), whom André Malraux considered to have priority as an "action painter" over Pollock, a claim that is probably not valid; however, André Masson who spent several years in America, definitely had a lasting influence on Pollock.

XXXIV. Tobey, "Forms Follow Man" (1941), tempera on cardboard

In Franz Kline's colossal black and white paintings a sense of power takes the place of Pollock's fluid action. This singularly American gesture has undoubtedly stimulated contemporary Japanese painters to revive evocative calligraphic sign-pictures. Kline does not use calligraphy or ornamental shapes—what he gives us is the overpowering reality of black forms charged with energy, restrained by the limits of the canvas yet straining beyond them. His paintings are concentrated statements of a vital impetus exerting itself within the limited area of the canvas.

The most radical innovations in painting are those in which the canvas is torn, tattered, and burnt. These effects create a layer-like surface peculiar to the relief, as well as an aggressive symbol of pain for "wounded man in a wounded world" (Haftmann). This gesture of mutilation may be observed in the work of the Italian Alberto Burri (**XXXV**). Here we find the destruction of aesthetic values through art itself, a tendency that has parallels in contemporary literature. Art becomes a document of existence; its formal qualities are only incidental. The novelty is not in the content of the statement, but in the fact that the statement is made in a completely nonrepresentational way. Burri may serve as the exponent of a large group of abstract artists who fight, with the instruments of art, against the accepted role of art; that is, against its interpretive, liberative, and redemptive roles. We must bear with and endure the monstrous horrors that attack us, for they mirror the specific dehumanization which has taken place in the twentieth century through technology, war, and political actions. These bizarre, grotesque, and monstrous elements also function as aesthetic play, as they have always done, except that, hitherto, the bizarre and the monstrous occupied only a subordinate place within a universal order that was based on religious or secular ethics.

And now Pop Art! On the surface it might seem a revival of Dada, but instead of being an art of revolt as Dada was, it is

a zestful affirmation of the bland banalities of Everyman's every-day commercial language. If one looks for the transformation of inner and outer experiences in art, he will find little here. The artist trusts the potential expressiveness of the object itself, but the plaster cake cannot be eaten, the Coca-Cola bottle does not afford "the pause that refreshes," the poster sells nothing but itself. Thus, the symbols of commercial and humdrum life occur merely as appearances and turn into undecipherable hieroglyph-ics. If skill and ingenuity, zest, fun, and despair are integral parts of an artist's creativity, then Pop Art is certainly creative. It constitutes a reaction against the ill-controlled and esoteric action of abstract expressionism. It reaffirms concreteness and precision; it advocates an open-eyed response to those aspects of daily life that are so obvious as to be barely visible; it occasionally shows wit and imagination in the selection and recomposition of its images. Its desolation is that of a world bustling with life and barren of meaning. Like the mirror, it does not comment on the image, but rather permits the image to comment on itself.

Nonrepresentational art: its achievement

We may subdivide the painting of abstract expressionism in vari-ous ways, but since it postulates its own reality and its own prob-lems, we cannot actually anticipate it through our points of view. As the American critic Leo Steinberg has said, "It is from an analysis of what the picture does to him that the critic learns what the picture actually succeeds in doing; and this knowledge alone leads to a definition of what problem is solved." [43]

For the time being, we have to beg the layman's understandable question: What does the painting mean? It has no meaning in the sense that it does not point to something already known and familiar. Therefore we cannot define it in terms of firmly estab-ished concepts. To put it more positively, the appearance of the painting is its own meaning. Its colored spaces, planes, rhythms, and contrasts are its statement. Its structure is identical with the process that gives it structure, and its truth is contained in the alternation between the artist's surrender to and control over his work.

The proportion of good abstract painting to bad is the same as the proportion of good to bad naturalistic painting. Yet we cannot any longer arrive at a value judgment by entrusting ourselves to a painting's familiar content.

Today form is its own content, or at least the bridge that leads to content. If by form we mean a modification of expression, then abstract form is not always even that, for sometimes it is *only* expression, only a diagram of vitality. Under the most favorable conditions, the mere expression of vitality may in itself be inspiring or uplifting, but at the same time we must recognize that it not only lacks an object, it lacks content, too. There arises the danger that egotistical inbreeding may deprive both artist and spectator of the world as material for art.

The new Prometheus makes his world. It is an independent, an "absolute" world, but the question arises whether it can be as comprehensive, as rich in universal content, as an art that refers to defined ideas and familiar appearances. Kant, who more fully illuminated the relationship between subject and object than any thinker before him, saw this problem and expressed it in terms of an impressive image: "The weightless dove, feeling the resistance of the air through which it flies, might well conceive the idea that it could fly even better in a total vacuum." [44]

This is the source of the deep uneasiness which we, as contemporaries, feel. The radical rejection of idea, model, and example and the replacement of them by self-developing formal design may well lead to a withering of all that art has done for mankind. Many of the products of abstract expressionism are egocentric, chaotic, culturally atrophied—is it enough that they are aesthetic creations? The best interpreters of this art, Werner

Haftmann and Herbert Read, have seen this danger and spoken of it.

On the positive side may be noted, once more, the liberation of art, the infinite expansion of the possibilities for expression and, most of all, the fact that nonrepresentational art is today practised everywhere. The fact of its existence proves the necessity of its existence. It is a genuine expression of what is good and what is evil in the record of our century. In this art the creative vitality of our age is alive; its vision may one day become the conventional vision of a later epoch. Its aesthetic boundlessness corresponds to our fluctuating, infinite image of the universe, and the meaning it conveys will become the building blocks of the future.

It is right that we should make up our minds about political and ethical systems, that we should either accept or reject them. But when it comes to the aesthetic statements of a period, we can only empathize with them or exclude ourselves from them. To mediate, to further such empathy and sympathy, is the intention of this book.

NOTES

1. Joseph Gantner, *Schicksale des Menschenbildes* (Berne, 1958), p. 139. (This and all subsequent translations, unless otherwise indicated, have been translated specifically for this book.)
2. Albert Wolff used this phrase in connection with the paintings of Cézanne at the Second Impressionist show of 1876, in *Figaro* (April 3, 1876).
3. Louis Sullivan, "Ornament in Architecture," in *Kindergarten Chats and Other Writings* (New York, 1947), p. 187.
4. Quoted in Wend Fischer, *Bau, Raum, Gerät* (Munich, 1957), p. 78.
5. Mies van der Rohe, quoted in Will Grohmann, *Zwischen den beiden Kriegen. Bildende Kunst, Architektur* (Frankfurt, 1953), p. 479.
6. Le Corbusier quoted in *ibid.*, p. 485.
7. San Francisco is presently entering a decisive phase in the battle between partial destruction of the Bay by commercial fill and the preservation plan upheld by planners and enlightened citizens.
   Other university cities which have become true monuments of contemporary architecture are those in Mexico City, Caracas, and Rio de Janeiro. That in Mexico City (1950-   ) is probably the most imaginative of its

kind. There a city of learning has been built on the barren ground of an old lava field, and a project dedicated to all the arts has achieved a creative combination of tradition and modernity. On the other hand, a traditional campus, such as that of Harvard University, has been both improved and disrupted by the insertion of excellent but incongruous modern buildings designed by Gropius, Le Corbusier, and others.

8. Walter Gropius, *The New Architecture and the Bauhaus* (New York, 1936), p. 27.
9. *Ibid.*, p. 23.
10. G. K. Chesterton, *Robert Browning* (New York, 1903), p. 99.
11. For a similar statement see J. J. Sweeney, *Joan Miró* (New York, 1941), p. 13.
12. This design is reproduced in Reed and Martin, *Gabo* (Cambridge, Mass., 1957), plates 47-49.
13. Guillaume Apollinaire, *Les Peintres cubistes* (Paris, 1913), p. 12.
14. *Picasso* (Paris, ed. Flouy, 1930; Eng. ed., 1939).
15. Henri Bergson, *Introduction to Metaphysics*, translated by T. E. Hulme (New York, 1911), p. 9.
16. Albert Gleizes and Jean Metzinger, *Du Cubisme* (Paris, 1912), p. 11. This essay is included in *Modern Artists on Art: Pioneer Twentieth-Century Essays*, ed. by Robert L. Herbert (Englewood Cliffs, N.J., Spectrum Books, 1964).
17. Juan Gris, "On the Possibilities of Painting" (1924), in Daniel Kahnweiler, *Juan Gris* (New York, 1947), p. 142.
18. A letter from Marc to his publisher in 1908, published in Klaus Lankheit, *Franz Marc* (Berlin, 1950), p. 18.
19. Quoted from the "Technical Manifesto of Futurist Painting, April 11, 1910," in Joshua Taylor, *Futurism* (New York, 1961), p. 126.
20. C. Carrà, "La Pittura dei Suoni, Rumori e Odori," in *Archivi del Futurismo* (Rome, 1958), Vol. I, p. 74.
21. Wassily Kandinsky, *Concerning the Spiritual in Art* (New York, 1947), p. 34.
22. Quoted in Walter Hess, *Dokumente zum Verständnis der modernen Malerei* (Hamburg, 1958), p. 66.
23. Quoted in Hess, *ibid.*, p. 98.
24. Piet Mondrian, *Neue Gestaltung* (Munich, 1925), p. 32.
25. Max Jacob, *L'Art poétique* (Paris, 1922), p. 67.
26. Quoted in Hess, *op. cit.*, p. 101.

27. This juxtaposition was made by Alfred H. Barr in *Cubism and Abstract Art* (New York, 1936), p. 157.
28. An English translation is *The New Vision* (New York, 1949).
29. Quoted from Klee's diaries in W. Grohmann, *Paul Klee* (New York, 1958), p. 95.
30. André Breton, *What is Surrealism?* (London, 1936).
31. James Thrall Soby, *Salvador Dali* (New York, 1946), p. 24.
32. Max Ernst, *Beyond Painting* (New York, 1948), p. 19.
33. André Breton, *op. cit.*, p. 25.
34. Gertrude Stein, *Picasso* (London, 1938), p. 43.
35. "Statement by Picasso: 1923," in *Picasso: Forty Years of his Art* (New York, 1939), p. 10.
36. *Ibid.*, p. 10.
37. André Breton, *op. cit.*, p. 17.
38. Werner Haftmann, *Painting in the Twentieth Century* (New York, 1960), p. 283.
39. *The Intimate Journals of Baudelaire*, translated by Christopher Isherwood (Boston, 1947), p. 10.
40. Juan Gris, "Notes on my Painting," in Kahnweiler, *op. cit.*, p. 138.
41. Leo Steinberg, *Arts* (April 1956), 52.
42. Picasso, *Wort und Bekenntnis* (Berlin, 1957), p. 22.
43. Leo Steinberg, *op. cit.*, p. 44.
44. Immanuel Kant, *Critique of Pure Reason*. Ed. August Messer, Berlin. Vol. III, p. 32.

INDEX